Journey to the Eye of the Storm

First published in Great Britain 1997
Lynx Communications/Anglican Renewal Ministries
Society for Promoting Christian Knowledge
Holy Trinity Church
Marylebone Road
London NW1 4DU

Copyright © David Beales 1997

Scripture quotations in this book are taken from the Revised Standard Version of the Bible, copyrighted © 1973 by the Division of Christian Education of the National Council of the Churches of Christ in the USA and from the New International Version of the Bible, copyrighted © 1973, 1978, 1984 by the International Bible Society and published by Hodder & Stoughton. Some Scripture quotations in Unit 4 are translated from *Edicio Revista E Atualizada No Brasil*, published by the Bible Society of Brazil, 1969.

All rights reserved. No part of this book may be reproduced or transmitted in any form or by any means, electronic or mechanical, including photocopying, recording, or by any information storage and retrieval system, without permission in writing from the publisher.

British Library Cataloguing-in-Publication Data
A catalogue record of this book is available from the British Library

ISBN 0-901443-02-7

Typeset by David Benham, Norwich
Printed in Great Britain by Hobbs the Printers, Southampton

Journey to the Eye of the Storm

*A training course for
young people on the Holy Spirit*

Mentor's Guide

David Beales

Contents

A letter to the minister
and church leadership team v

Introduction 1

UNIT 1
'Body-building':
Building the group
and getting started 9

UNIT 2
'A jamming session':
Growing in harmony! 14

UNIT 3
'Get drenched!': How
to be filled with the Spirit 18

UNIT 4
Pneumatic drills!
(A) Gifts of tongues,
interpretation and prophecy 24

UNIT 5
Pneumatic drills!
(B) Gifts of healing, faith
and miracles 31

UNIT 6
Pneumatic drills!
(C) Gifts of wisdom,
knowledge and discernment 40

UNIT 7
The Tertius Diaries 49

UNIT 8
Chaos in Corinth 59

UNIT 9
Crazy mirror or
God's mirror? The
Holy Spirit and self-image 62

UNIT 10
'You are gifted!' Identifying,
owning and developing
natural and spiritual gifts 69

UNIT 11
'Tell the story!':
(A) Preparation for
the group's presentation 73

UNIT 12
'Tell the story!':
(B) The presentation 74

A letter to the minister and church leadership teams

Dear Friends,

Journey to the Eye of the Storm has been designed for young people to lead each other, in the company of adult mentors. The young people who have been through the journey will have had a taste of ministry to, with and from one another. They follow a long line of young people who have been called by God to active ministry.

Throughout the history of the Bible, God chose and gifted young people. Young women such as Mary the mother of Jesus, Esther the queen, the four prophet-daughters of Philip; young men such as Joseph the dreamer, David the king, Jeremiah the prophet. All were called by God when they were young and were given special abilities for the tasks they had to do.

Peter preached on the Day of Pentecost, 'God says I will pour out my Spirit on all people. Your sons and your daughters will prophesy, your young men will see visions...' (We're quite sure he meant that young women were included in this last statement since he went on to say, 'Even on my servants both men and women, I will pour out my Spirit.')

Young people today are being called and gifted by God to serve him in today's world. *Journey to the Eye of the Storm* has taken them deeper into God and given them the opportunity to exercise gifts and skills of ministry. They will have learned that they are called to serve, not merely by being told so, but by being thrust into ministries of witness and service. They will have gone some way towards recognizing and developing their own giftings and will have experienced the grace and presence of God guiding, directing and empowering them. They will have developed as a community and will have been encouraged to look outwards, seeking ways to reach out to others.

In short, they have been treated as creators rather than consumers of ministry. In the Church, we have often seen young people as recipients of ministry; youth ministry has referred to that which is done by adults for, to (and occasionally with) young people. However, in contrast to current western values which push the individual towards looking after 'number one' as top priority, the Church needs more than ever to encourage young people into sacrificial service, for this is the character of discipleship.

In preparing *Journey to the Eye of the Storm*, I have consciously sought to nurture an attitude of humility, encouraging people to receive God's gifts for the purpose of service. I believe that young people will need further encouragement and incentive for service in the hope that they will soon be so captivated by the desire and thrill of serving Jesus in the power of the Spirit that they'll never look back, but will move forward into a lifetime of effective ministry. For this, I urge you to consider how the Church might continue to nurture the ministries of these young people.

In my ministry with young people, I have found that there are 3 components of effective learning:

1 Enabling young people to become aware of the needs of the world and the call of Christ.
2 Giving young people the opportunity to discuss thoroughly the issues that have been brought to their attention and to offer their feedback. For example, it is not enough just to show young people examples of poverty or suffering; they need opportunity to talk out their feelings and response in the context of a safe peer group.
3 Giving young people opportunities for service. Young people thrive on being given responsibility. Of course they will make mistakes, but offering them responsibility so often brings the best out of them.

It is these values that are reflected in *Journey to the Eye of the Storm*, a course, which is interactive and gives the young people plenty of opportunity to learn, to put into practice what they are learning and to take responsibility for leadership not only in their small group, but as they plan and present a celebration which tells their stories at the end of the course.

It is my hope that the local church will participate in this act of encouraging and releasing young people into ministry. I hope that you will meet with those who have been through *Journey to the Eye of the Storm* to discern together the next stage in moving the young people on towards maturity in ministry and service.

With every blessing for the task ahead

Yours sincerely

David Beales

Introduction

Young people and the Church

Young people are God's agents for the renewal of the Church. Young people often have the enthusiasm, passion and sense of fun that adults may have lost. A church without the fervour and insights of young people may die because 'Where there is no vision the people perish.'

Aims of the journey

Journey to the Eye of the Storm seeks to enable young people:
1 To be catalysts of renewal for one another. As a result, the whole church will be renewed and its mission strengthened.
2 To live lives filled with God's Spirit. The journey treats young people as creators not consumers, as participants with God in his work today, as people gifted with grace and able to exercise ministry fully within and beyond the Church.
3 To receive, develop and exercise the gifts of the Spirit described in 1 Corinthians, to produce the fruits of the Spirit described in Galatians and to be fired with a passion for Jesus.

The principles behind *Journey to the Eye of the Storm*

About the Bible
1 Scripture is story; in a universal sense the Christian Scriptures tell the story of God's dealings with humanity. In a personal sense, the stories of Scripture illuminate and reveal the nature of an individual's life story.
2 When the Christian community enters into Scripture as story, the individual lives and the corporate life of the community are enriched.
3 Imaginative engagement with the Bible invites an inner response which requires some form of concrete articulation.
4 Both Evangelism and Christian Nurture include an invitation to individuals and communities to enter imaginatively into the drama of the biblical story.

5 The biblical teaching on the Holy Spirit is not a matter for mere objective assessment; it carries the implicit mandate that we recognize Jesus as Lord and give our lives to him.

About discipleship
1 Christian discipleship is lived in community. A disciple cannot be a loner.
2 The Kingdom of God is inclusive in character; therefore, the church needs to be an open, accessible community, particularly with regard to the unchurched.
3 The ministry and witness of young Christian people need to be encouraged and nurtured by supportive leadership.
4 Everyone has a hunger for a real encounter with God.
5 Individuals may be addressed by the Word of God in the presence of a group gathered around the Bible. There is the possibility of a dynamic encounter with God, in a group context, which will have far-reaching effects in an individual's life.

THE CONTEXT

The context of the journey is a group of young people leading one another in the company of caring and mature adult mentors. Depending on the size of the group, it will normally be important to have 3 or 4 mentors. One mentor to three or four young people is a good ratio. A mentoring married couple is particularly recommended. This provides a sense of parenting and a model of marriage. The recommended size of the group is between 7 and 21. If there are more than 21, have concurrent older and younger groups operating on the same timetable; the weekend can be done together.

The mentors will help to motivate the group, introducing the activities during the first session and the weekend. However, the more usual role will be to assist the young people in preparing and planning the weekly gatherings. The local church fellowship is the broader context from which the young people will be recruited for the journey.

THE LOCAL CHURCH'S ROLE

The church family will travel with the journeyers as prayer-partners. In this way the whole church family will be engaged in the journey. Inter-generational relationships will be enhanced and the contributions of young people to the life of the church will be encouraged.

The task of mentoring

The mentors will help to navigate their group through the course. In the process they will form relationships with individuals in the group and will assist them in presenting parts of the course and in responding to God's prompting. They will have previous knowledge of the biblical chapters concerned and previous experience of the gifts of the Holy Spirit.

They will need to be familiar with the activities, biblical passages and purpose of the journey. Reading this manual with understanding is one thing; however, it's better to have practised some of the activities beforehand. This will inspire confidence and enable mentors to know how to motivate the group to participate and how to support the presenters of each session or activity. It is recommended that the team of mentors meets together beforehand to prepare, discuss the journey and pray together.

WORKSHOP TIPS FOR MENTORS

In order to build leadership skills and confidence in the group, certain members will be invited to lead Units 2–6, 9 and 11/12 with assistance from the mentors. (Units 7, 8 and 10 are processes which the mentors should lead. For Units 11/12, the leader's task is to co-ordinate and present the act of witness that concludes the journey.) Group members may lead individually or in pairs. Mentors will workshop each of the presentations led by members of the group. This will require the leader or pair of leaders to meet with the mentor and go through how they will present the Unit.

The aim of having young people lead the sessions is twofold:
1 To develop their skills in leading and speaking about faith.
2 To encourage the others to listen with rapt attention to one of their peers presenting.

Clearly, the task of presenting a unit will require preparation in the form of study, prayer and discussion. The mentor's role is to support, encourage and develop the young presenter and to ensure that the content and objectives of the unit are covered. Careful workshopping will build the confidence of the young people, enabling them to be effective and faithful witnesses. It will also ensure that misunderstandings and wrong doctrines are dealt with before the meetings; it's much better to deal with them privately rather than interrupt the presenter during the meeting to correct a statement. Such an interruption may be taken as a put-down, discouraging the young person from wanting ever to lead another session!

The following steps are recommended:

1 Assign responsibility for Units 2, 3, 4, 5, 6, 9 and 11/12 as soon as possible. Units 1, 7, 8 and 10 are best directed by a mentor. Pairs or threes make take responsibility for a unit, dividing up the different sections accordingly. However, this does make the mentor's task two or three times as arduous. In pairs or threes, some who are less confident may act in support roles and have responsibility for sharing in the preparation and praying for the presenter during the session.
2 Set a date with the presenter to go through how the unit will be led. We call this The Workshop. The presenter agrees to read through all the material for the unit beforehand.
3 At the workshop, the presenter's role is to demonstrate an understanding of the content and process of the unit. The mentor's role is to affirm the presenter and ensure that the unit will be led carefully. There is also opportunity to develop the spiritual life of the presenter there and then. For instance, if there is a pair of presenters leading Unit 3 who have never been filled with the Spirit, pray with them to be filled during the workshop; enable them to experience the Spirit's gifts then and there so that they have a testimony to draw on before the meeting.
4 Encourage presenters to draw on experience and illustrations to make a point. On a practical level ensure that they have marked any biblical references clearly so that they can allude to them quickly and efficiently during the meeting. Share your own story with the presenter to encourage personal sharing.
5 The workshop is a great opportunity for ministry at a personal level. Pray for the encounter beforehand that it will be a moment of God's presence for both mentor and presenter.

The Journal

A journal traces a journey. During *Journey to the Eye of the Storm* participants are relating the information they are discovering to their spiritual journeys. As they debrief all the different activities, they will be asked to consider how the stories, ideas and concepts are relevant to their experience today.

In addition to the weekly activities, printed in the Journal are 31 readings about the activity of the Holy Spirit in the Old and New Testaments. Space is given to record responses to these readings as well. Unit 2 provides a practical opportunity to get started with the Journal.

The Journal is to encourage participants to record their experiences, insights, questions, doubts, discoveries and memories. Learning is taking place at various levels. At head level, information about the Holy Spirit is being presented and processed. At heart level, everybody is making a personal response to the activities and the group; the biblical stories and characters are coming to life, bringing surprises and a whole range of emotions with which the participants are asked to identify. Spiritually, the Word of God is becoming 'living and active, sharper than a two-edged sword'; the Holy Spirit is making an appeal to the mind and the heart as the group dives into the Word of God.

All this is so valuable that it is worth recording. The Journal then becomes a record of the spiritual journey in which the whole person is involved. When everyone is together, the most appropriate time for doing the Journal activity is during and after the Debriefs, which conclude each activity. Allow 3 to 5 minutes' time. Some may not want to do this at all; others will want to go on for longer.

Some groups of young people may feel that the Journal is being imposed like homework! Gently encourage, but don't push it as a compulsory activity. Assure participants that nobody else will read the Journal. Be prepared for some surprises; some may want to do stacks of writing. Journals are entirely confidential, unless someone chooses to share what they have recorded.

It is helpful to put on some ambient music as a background to the Journal time. There's no problem with people talking to one another about what they want to include. However, see the Journal time as an expression of prayer in which each person is recording a little of what God is saying to them through the activities and content of the gathering.

Here are some prompt questions for those doing the Journal which may be suggested to encourage recording:

- What was the last activity?
- What did I do?
- What did I discover? About the Holy Spirit? About my own belief?
- How did I feel?
- What was the point of it?
- What about the other people I'm with? How did they find the activity?
- Is this relevant to my life?

It is important for the mentors to set an example and participate in doing the Journal throughout the course. Each mentor should own and use the Journal and be open enough to say how they are using it (while keeping it confidential). Feel free to say if you failed to do it as well; but then feel free next time to say you're catching up!!

Prayer-partners

To involve the whole Christian community in *Journey to the Eye of the Storm*, members of the church (or churches) which is sponsoring the event will be invited to be prayer-partners of individual participants. They will be invited to pray each day for a named individual and to offer encouragement in the form of a letter to be delivered when participants embark on the process. This communicates the sense of importance and value being placed on the activity. Each participant will know that he/she is part of a wider community; Christian disciples do not journey alone. Those seeking for truth may likewise have partners during their exploration.

The co-ordinator should invite prayerful people to deliver a letter to a named individual in a sealed envelope before *Journey to the Eye of the Storm* begins. A brief summary of the process and an invitation to participate as prayer-partners is included below; this may be copied for distribution to those who will pray and write a letter.

> *Journey to the Eye of the Storm* is designed to help people explore together the person and work of the Holy Spirit. Each person is brought face to face with the biblical accounts of the Holy Spirit and their importance for our lives. The activities enable Christian people to grow deeper in faith, to experience the Holy Spirit and to exercise the gifts of the Spirit, according to the principles of 1 Corinthians 12—14.
>
> It is important for every participant to know that they are not alone during this exercise. The Spirit wants to meet all of us in genuine depth. Therefore, we would like each participant to have a prayer supporter for the duration of the process. We would like you to commit yourself to pray daily for one person for the duration of the exercise and to write a letter of encouragement to be distributed at the beginning. Participants will be encouraged to communicate with you at the end, either by way of a visit, letter or phone call. You will also be invited to a presentation by the whole group at the end of the process.
>
> Thank you for giving this some consideration. Please let us know if you'd like to be involved in this way.

A note about music and worship

Throughout the manual, no music or time of singing has been recommended. However, this should not prevent you from using music worship during the meetings. Musical tastes are so diverse and knowledge of songs is so varied that it would be presumptuous to prescribe the music that should be used. If your group is comfortable about singing together, there is ample scope for worship during the times of prayer and ministry – indeed, music worship is highly recommended as a means of drawing into God's presence. The weekly sessions are 100 minutes in length; if you meet for 2 hours on a Friday or Saturday night, there is room for 15–20 minutes' singing.

Units 9–11 will be a particularly good time for encouraging musical creativity, if the resources and giftedness in the group allow.

A note about 1 Corinthians 14.33–36

Sooner or later someone will raise the question about women speaking in church. It is not the place of this manual to develop a detailed interpretation of this passage. Mentors should ensure that they understand the issues involved in interpreting this text and are prepared to discuss them when appropriate. It is recommended that mentors discuss the issue amongst themselves and with their minister.

The author's view on interpreting this text has briefly been summarized below. This is inadequate as a full explanation of issues surrounding the place of women in the church and the interpretation of the whole of Paul's first letter to the Corinthians, but it may be a helpful starting-point for the discussion.

Paul prohibits the Corinthian women from speaking in the public gatherings. In the historical and cultural context of ancient Corinth, it would have done damage to the credibility of Christianity for women to have taken on the role of teachers in the church. In our present western cultural context women are recognized as perfectly competent teachers and public speakers. Today, there is nothing immodest or improper about women addressing people of both sexes. Hence, the cultural principle on which Paul based his strict censure of women speaking in church has been removed.

A note about confirmation

The rite of confirmation in the Anglican Church is a channel through which God strengthens his people with the Holy Spirit in response to the Bishop's prayer and laying on of hands. Confirmation is affirmed whether it is done before or after *Journey to the Eye of the Storm*.

If someone has been confirmed previously without any visible manifestation of the Holy Spirit or without being able to operate the spiritual gifts, their receiving and operating the gifts during the course of *Journey to the Eye of the Storm* demonstrate God's activity in reponse to the Bishop's prayer, 'Confirm, O Lord, your servant with your Holy Spirit.' There has merely been a delayed reaction between the Bishop's prayer and the candidate's response.

On the other hand, some confirmation candidates will already have been through the activities of *Journey to the Eye of the Storm* and will have been filled with the Spirit, free to operate the Spirit's gifts effectively. In this case, the rite of confirmation is an outward, public act formalizing what has happened already in the candidate's life. Since the confirmation candidate asserts and renews baptismal vows personally and publicly, it is recommended that unconfirmed people who have completed *Journey to the Eye of the Storm* proceed to confirmation as soon as is reasonably possible. Indeed, the journey may be used as part of the confirmation preparation process.

UNIT 1

'Body-building': Building the group and getting started

> Aim: To build relationships and trust within the group according to the biblical model of the Body of Christ. To encourage group members to make commitments to each other to phone or visit in order to pray for one another.

In the first 2 sessions we need to enable each person to feel valued and therefore to grow in confidence. They've got to become like a band of jamming musicians able to relate to one another. They have to be able to listen to one another, take a lead, give a lead to someone else. They need to be able to trust one another and take responsibility in the group, so these initial sessions must form them into a group which is cohesive and aware of its aims and function.

That implies:
- each person motivated to participate in achieving the goals of the course;
- each person able to be assertive and listen to one another;
- each person willing to take responsibility within the group;
- each person confident to communicate at mouth, head and heart level.

The particular aims of this session are:

A To create a safe and happy environment.
B To create group cohesion.
C To communicate the objectives of *Journey to the Eye of the Storm*.
D To develop an understanding of and feeling for Paul's model of the Body of Christ.

AIM A

To create a safe and happy environment

20 minutes

If the group members already know each other, this activity should be fairly brief. If, on the other hand, they don't know each other at all, time should be taken now to help them get to know each other. Spend time finding out what different people in the group like to do; encourage them to express how they feel about their participation in *Journey to the Eye of the Storm*.

9

Play any getting-to-know-you games that are appropriate. For instance:
- invite people to say their names and one word to describe them which should begin with the same letter as their name;
- invite people to say one thing that they've done which nobody else in the group will know about.

AIM B

To create group cohesion

20 minutes

Explain that the group will be working together for several weeks so it's important to establish good working relationships and to bring out the best in everyone. Together, choose a name which says something about the group's corporate personality. Find out each person's interests and skills and talk about the image of *Journey to the Eye of the Storm*. Write the chosen name on a big piece of card or butcher's paper; someone with artistic skills can be chosen to do this. Then invite everyone in the group to write or draw their names, signatures or logos. The resulting poster can be displayed every time you meet to encourage the sense of community and cohesion.

AIM C

To communicate the objectives of *Journey to the Eye of the Storm*

15 minutes

What are we here for?
1 To grow in friendship with one another, by creating a co-operative group.
2 To grow in understanding, by investigating the Bible, discussing and learning from one another.
3 To grow in skills and giftings for ministry, by receiving God's Spirit and the gifts he brings, and by hosting an event at the end to tell the story of what happens to us through the journey to friends, relatives, colleagues.

Explain how most of the sessions will be led by the members of the group and describe the workshop process. Depending on the number of people in the group, allocate either an individual or pair or threesome to take responsibility for the 7 different sessions – these include Units 2–6, 9 and 10–12 – with assistance from the mentors. (Units 1, 7, 8 are processes which the mentors should lead. For Units 10–12, the task is to co-ordinate and present the act of witness that concludes the journey.)

AIM D

To develop an understanding of and feeling for Paul's model of the Body of Christ in 1 Corinthians 12.12–27

25 minutes

'The body is a unit, though it is made up of many parts; and though all its parts are many, they form one body. So it is with Christ.'

Your group must create a body. (If there are more than 8 people in the group you will need to create more than one body.) This body needs:
- A mouth
- A hand
- An eye/ear (may be separate or one person)
- Feet (unlimited number, preferably at least three)

The group decides who will play each part of the body. The feet have to carry others so it is recommended that they are the heaviest!

NB: The different parts of the body may only do what those body parts normally do. They are not allowed to do anything else. Thus:
- Only the eye may see.
- Only the hand may do manual actions.
- Only the mouth may eat or drink.
- Only the feet may walk – thus they have to carry the other parts of the body in response to the instructions.
- The ear and the eye may speak to pass on instructions, since ears and eyes transmit messages to the brain.
- The body must be connected up.

When decisions have been taken about who will play each part, the eye/ear goes to the co-ordinator who gives an instruction for the body. Once the instruction has been communicated to the rest of the group, the body wakes up and begins to function to complete the task given by the co-ordinator.

The co-ordinator will tell the ear (or each of the ears) that the body must walk a distance of 30 metres. At that point the hand will give the mouth a drink. Cups of water will have been placed at a distance of 30 metres. (The distance may be less if you have to do the activity indoors.) The ear must pass on the instruction to the rest of the body. The feet must carry the other parts of the body, guided by the eye. Then the hand, guided by the eye, must pick up the cup and enable the mouth to drink.

DEBRIEF AND CONCLUSION

20 minutes

When the activity has been completed (and people have been dried off) get everybody to sit down together again to debrief. It is important to ask questions after this activity to check that learning has taken place from the experience and to review what it felt like to be the different parts of the body.

- Ask each part of the body how it felt to have to take responsibility to perform the role assigned.
- Check who was the mouth in each group; ask if the mouths got wet or were able to drink easily.
- Check who was the eye in each group; ask how the eyes felt about the ability of the rest of the body to listen to directions and follow them.
- Check who were the feet and hands in each group.
- Ask what other learning or discovery has been made.
- Refer back to 1 Corinthians 12 and talk about participation and responsibility within the group.

We are a mini-expression of the Body of Christ. It's important that we keep connected to one another during this journey, because we're travelling together. The ingredients of love described in that chapter are important for us. There's no room for backbiting, excluding people or forming cliques. It is never easy to be a community because people get on one another's nerves from time to time. However, we're a temporary community at least for a few weeks, so we're going to commit ourselves to help and encourage one another like the players in a team sport. Let's agree each to choose one other person to pray for and encourage this week. Maybe a phone call or a visit during the week to assure the other person of your prayers would be encouraging. There are other people praying for you, too.

At this point distribute the letters from members of the church and invite people to open them and read them for a few minutes. Invite people to express how they feel on reading their letter. Mention that it will be important to visit their adult prayer-partner at some point to say how they're going during, or at the end of, the journey.

When the time is up, conclude with some prayer. You may have already established a habitual form of praying that makes everyone in the group feel comfortable and relaxed. If you haven't, or if you'd like to try a different way of praying together, here's a method that has been developed by the young people of Shal Church in Grimsby. Have a Bible ready to pass round the group.

The Bible is God's Word speaking to us; our prayers are in response to God's desire to be our friend. Holding the Bible while praying becomes a sign of both listening and speaking. Each person may mention something that you are thankful for and/or something you would like to ask God for. You are not expected to reveal personal details; if there are personal problems you would like to mention to God, you can simply say, 'P. P.'! Hold the Bible up while you speak, then pass it to the next person when you have finished. If you choose not to say anything, simply pass the Bible on to the next person. Everyone focuses on the person holding the Bible and is praying with them. You don't need to close your eyes or say words that are peculiar to you.

When the last person has finished, the prayer time is over and the gathering is concluded. Invite everyone to take the Journal to read during the week and make sure they bring it next time, where there'll be some discussion about how to use it.

UNIT 2

'A jamming session': Growing in harmony!

Aim: To become a biblical community by motivating the journalling and further cementing the group around innovative, biblical activities.

REVIEW

15 minutes

- Ask people what they remember from last week's session
- Invite people to say how they got on during the week. Ask if anyone has read any of the readings in the Journal. Ask if anyone can remember any ideas, stories or insights that they'd like to share with the group. Don't be discouraged if nobody has anything to say. The second part of this session is designed to fix that!
- Ask how the prayer-partnerships have been.

BIBLE-JAMMING

40 minutes

The teaching of 1 Corinthians 13 is key to the whole process of the course. The attitude of love must be central to the approach that the participants bring to the course. The goal of the course is that they will show the fruits of the Spirit, the first of which is love.

In order further to bond the group together, the group will be invited to 'jam' the chapter. 'Jamming' is especially appropriate to the poetic passages of the Bible and 1 Corinthians 13 may have been based on an early Christian song. In groups of 5–8 people, do the following:

1 Introduce the jam session.

> We are going to jam this passage so as to be able to hear it in an unusual way. When musicians come together to jam, they have to listen carefully and sensitively to one another and they have to express their music in such a way as both to blend in with everyone else and to make a unique contribution to the overall sound. Sometimes one instrument will take on the tune, so that it is heard above the rest; sometimes a theme that was played earlier will be

featured again; sometimes there may be all instruments playing, sometimes only one or two. Jamming musicians create a unique sound but they never know what it's going to be until they give it a go. We'll go through a process to help us jam this passage and then listen to the outcome and see what surprises us.

2 Sit on the floor in a circle. Read the passage verse by verse around the circle.

Everybody will have been wondering when it was their turn. I bet most of you counted up how many verses were to be read before you and then you figured out which bit to look at so you didn't listen to everyone else's reading! This time, the person reading will stop at any point and the next person will pick up where the text was left.

3 Now re-read the chapter around the circle again. However, this time the reader stops at any point and gives the reading to the next person, who picks it up and continues until he/she chooses to stop.

4 Third time round the text is read around the circle again, except that this time the reading is taken by the next person in turn. The first person begins, but the second person takes it on when he/she chooses to, and so on until the passage has been read.

Now we are ready for full jamming. Jamming is about giving and receiving the words, listening to one another and making our own unique contribution as well. You will need to be aware of what everyone else is saying, giving and receiving the text yourself. Sometimes you will be quiet and sometimes you will be speaking. You may want to return to an earlier part of the passage and re-read something; when you are jamming the order may change. Jamming musicians will pick up a theme or a tune and keep returning to it from time to time. 'Louds' and 'softs' should be varied. Some words or phrases need to come out loudly, others will be said more softly.

5 Now the group is ready for full jamming. Allow the jamming reading to go on as long as it needs to. Repeat it if you like.

Debrief:
- Invite people to say what they heard that was fresh, surprising and new.
- Encourage them to say why they chose to emphasize certain words or phrases.

- Ask for at least one practical application from each of the 'love' statements; what do these statements mean for our relationships with family, neighbours, friends and members of this group?
- Ask what the difference is between the idea of love as expressed in this chapter compared with popular ideas of love as found in teenage magazines, romance novels and movies.

TAKE A BREAK

10 minutes

Allow people a 5-minute break because they've been concentrating hard on jamming. Everyone should get up and walk around or stretch, to be ready to listen carefully to one another again in a while.

During the break set up the room so as to encourage a quieter time of listening to God. You might like to light candles (but make sure people can still see), or put on some ambient music in the background. Show that you expect a different mood.

JOURNAL TIME

30 minutes

Ensure everyone has their Journal.

Everyone knows that a relationship needs time. Time for people to get to know each other. Time away from everyone else. Time to learn how to communicate. Time to listen. Time to speak. The idea of having a spiritual journal is to give us time to focus on our relationship with God.

We're going to do a journal time together so that when we're apart we'll be more clear about how to use the time effectively; to be skilled at entering the eye of the storm.

Turn to Acts 1.1–11. A promise of power.
- *React:* say the suggested prayer from one of the Psalms in the Journal introduction.
- *Read:* allow everyone time to glance through the passage again.
- *Reflect:* invite everyone to be as still and comfortable as possible; take a minute or so to be quiet, to close the eyes and to breathe deeply in order to relax, then read the meditation to them slowly, allowing time for the imagination to delve into the scene.

Imagine you are there with the other disciples listening to Jesus. Look around and observe the scenery. What kind of day is it? Watch the faces of the others who are listening. What is their expression? Be aware of yourself. How do you feel, being there? How do the others accept you?

Listen to Jesus' words: 'Wait here to receive the promise from the Father which I told you about.' There's a promise for you. What do you feel like when a gift is promised? Here's the promise: 'John baptized you with water, but in a few days you will be baptized with the Holy Spirit.' Imagine John in his camel's hair garb ducking people right under the water until they are entirely immersed.

Remember what it feels like to go under water. How does the water feel all around you? 'When the Holy Spirit comes to you, you will receive power.' What does that mean to you? Imaging getting plugged in to a source of power. 'You will be my witnesses...' Imagine yourself in the witness box in court, answering questions about Jesus! And you're plugged in to the power source!

Suddenly, there's a cloud all around. Jesus is no longer there; he's being lifted into the sky! What does it look like? What about the expressions on the others' faces now? Two men in white are speaking to you. Another promise! He'll come back! How does that change the faces of the group? How do you feel? Rest with one of the pictures that's been in your mind. Stay there for a while...

Now open your eyes and be aware of one another again. Ask if anybody wants to share briefly what they were thinking about or what pictures came into their mind.

- *Reply:* encourage people to write (or draw) what they were thinking about. If they want to talk to one another about what they were thinking, that's fine. Or they can write a prayer in reply to the passage; or whatever comes to mind. Finally, draw everyone's attention to the Journal section, 'How to use the Journal and the readings – your personal retreat time'.

CONCLUSION

5 minutes

Tonight we've been practising how to become a biblical community; how to let the Word of God get into our system. Jamming and journalling are ways of listening to God by letting his words take root in our minds. Over the next week, keep up the journalling and ask that God will fill you with his Spirit each day. Next week we will claim Jesus' promise of the Holy Spirit.

Finally, close by praying together, either in your own way or in the Shal Church style, as suggested in Unit 1.

UNIT 3

'Get drenched!': How to be filled with the Spirit

Aims: To tell the stories of when the Holy Spirit came to people in Acts. To encourage people to be filled with the Holy Spirit.

PREPARATION

Several days before the gathering, invite 5 people from the group to be prepared to tell these 5 stories from Acts (one per person):

1 The Day of Pentecost; Acts 2.1–13.
2 Peter and John in Samaria; Acts 8.14–23.
3 Ananias and Saul; Acts 9.17–19.
4 Peter at the house of Cornelius; Acts 10.44–48.
5 Paul in Ephesus; Acts 19.1–7.

Jot down the 9 references from the 'How to be filled with the Holy Spirit' section on page 21 to distribute to various people when you arrive at that point. Arrange to have a whiteboard or a large sheet of blank paper available so that you can record the steps about how to be filled with the Holy Spirit.

Be well prepared, spiritually, for this session, making sure that those who are covering the course in prayer are aware that you will be praying for people to be filled with the Spirit. Give careful thought about how you will explain about speaking in tongues, and how you are going to lead the prayer and ministry for this. The notes are there to help and guide you, but do adapt this in the way that is going to best suit your group.

REVIEW AND INTRODUCTION

15 minutes

- Ask people what they remember from last week's session.
- Invite people to say how they got on during the week. Ask if anyone has read any of the readings in the Journal. Ask if anyone can remember any ideas, stories or insights that they'd like to share with the group.

- Ask how the prayer-partnerships have been.
- Remind everyone of the *Journey to the Eye of the Storm* idea.
- State the aims of the meeting, adding that there will be time later in the session to pray with one another for the infilling of the Holy Spirit.

The earliest Christians faced all kinds of storms. For a start, Jesus' close circle was devastated at the crucifixion; then they were over the moon at his resurrection. Their moods changed rapidly!

In their delight at knowing the risen Jesus, they frequently upset the religious and political authorities. On occasions, they were beaten, thrown in jail, stoned and had to run for their lives. These were the storms imposed from outside!

In addition, since the Christian Church was a brand new group, nobody really knew what the rules were – or if there were any rules. As a result, there were many disputes among the Christians. These were the storms that brewed up from within!

Nobody was perfect when the Holy Spirit came to the earliest Christians. Nor was life particularly easy and carefree. The Spirit was promised by Jesus and given by the Father. Read John 14.16 ... 'And I will ask the Father, and he will give you another Counsellor to be with you for ever – the Spirit of truth.'

THE HOLY SPIRIT IN ACTS

There are 5 incidents recorded in Acts of the coming of the Holy Spirit upon people. Let's take a look at these.

25 minutes

1 Ask someone to tell the Pentecost story, Acts 2.1–13. Thank them for their contribution.

This was a unique event. Beforehand the Holy Spirit had only been available occasionally to people. Now everyone who was a follower of Jesus could receive the Holy Spirit. See Acts 2.38–39. The infilling of the Holy Spirit meant that the disciples could 'speak in tongues' – Acts 2.4. An audible, outward sign. Wind and fire are emblems of the Holy Spirit.

2 Ask someone to tell the story of Peter and John in Samaria, Acts 8.14–23. Thank them for their contribution.

Simon saw some visible, outward effect of the infilling of the Spirit (v. 18). We're not sure what this was. Maybe the people spoke in tongues, maybe they shook or fell; we can't be certain, except that something was evident. Peter and John specifically prayed for the Samaritan Christians to receive the Holy Spirit. They laid hands on them as an outward sign of what God was doing inwardly.

3 Ask someone to tell the story of Paul's infilling with the Spirit. Acts 9.10–19. Thank them for their contribution.

Ananias placed his hands on Saul as he prayed for him to be filled with the Holy Spirit. His recovery from blindness was the immediate outward sign of his infilling with the Holy Spirit. We know that Saul (later renamed Paul) spoke with tongues because he said so in 1 Corinthians 14.18: 'I thank God that I speak in tongues more than all of you.'

EITHER

TAKE A BREAK

10 minutes

Take a few minutes' break to let the information sink in. Invite people to stand up, walk around, stretch for a while, then to form pairs or threes to ask one another,
'What have you heard so far?'
'What questions would you like to ask?'
If any questions emerge, let them be raised and discussed.

OR

JAM IT

10 minutes

If your group enjoyed the jamming activity last week have a go at jamming the next passage; go through the same 4-stage process as before (see Unit 2). It's a passage that lends itself to jamming because everybody spoke at once!

4 Ask someone to tell the story of Peter at the house of Cornelius, Acts 10.44–48. Thank them for their contribution. (Ignore this instruction if you've jammed it.)

Speaking in tongues and praising God was the visible evidence that the Holy Spirit had fallen on these people. The Spirit came on them just as on the disciples at Pentecost – see Acts 11.15, where Peter reports this incident: 'As I began to speak, the Holy Spirit came on them as he had come on us at the beginning.'

These people were Gentiles, not Jews. The implication is that you don't have to have a special upbringing to be given the Holy Spirit. As in Samaria, the gift of the Spirit followed the hearing of the Gospel about Jesus – in Samaria Philip told them, in Caesarea Peter told them.

5 Ask someone to read the story of the Ephesian people who received the Holy Spirit, Acts 19.1–7. Thank them for their contribution.

They'd only heard half the story. John the Baptist had told his audience that someone else was going to come who was greater than him – see Luke 3.16, where John told the crowd: 'I baptize you with water. But one more powerful than I will come, the thongs of whose sandals I am not worthy to untie. He will baptize you with the Holy Spirit and with fire.'

These people in Ephesus expected forgiveness, but had not experienced the Holy Spirit in person. They needed to be taught. Paul laid hands on them as he prayed. The visible outward evidence of the Spirit was that they spoke in tongues and prophesied.

APPLICATION

20 minutes

What about us? There are some things we can be sure of:

1 Every Christian has the Spirit in them – 1 Corinthians 12.3, Acts 2.39, John 3.5–6.
2 Many Christians, like the Ephesian 12, have not been taught about the Holy Spirit.
3 In the New Testament, as the 5 passages from Acts have shown, there is no doubt that visible evidence of the Spirit's effect on people was expected; very often speaking in tongues was the immediate outward sign. See also 1 Corinthians 12.7.
4 In the twentieth century, and particularly since the 1960s, many Christians have experienced the infilling of the Holy Spirit with effects similar to those described in Acts.

How to be filled with the Holy Spirit

Here is a step-by-step guide to being filled with the Holy Spirit. Write up each step on a whiteboard or sheet of butcher's paper as you go through the steps. The words in *italic* are the key words to write up. Distribute the references you have written down and invite different people to look up and read the various verses as they are mentioned.

1 *Confess*: it is clear that we have to be open to God. Therefore we have to confess where we've gone wrong and get rid of any blockage. Read Psalm 66.18.
2 *Thank God for forgiveness* on the basis of what Jesus has done to remove our guilt (1 Peter 2.24).
3 *Believe you have been forgiven* (1 John 1.9).
4 *Ask God to fill you with his Spirit.* You can be sure that he wants to do this because:
(a) Jesus has promised the Spirit, John 14.26.
(b) Jesus has assured us that the Father wants to give us his Spirit (Luke 11.11–13).
5 *Agree* with two other people on this prayer and be sure that God is going to do what you ask (Matthew 18.20).
6 *Receive* (John 20.22). Picture something from the Gospels in your mind; perhaps Jesus on the cross, or meeting the risen Jesus in the garden on Easter Sunday. Make a choice to receive the gift of the Holy Spirit. It's no good going into a shop to buy a loaf of bread if you don't receive the loaf of bread and take it with you out of the shop (or an ice-cream or anything else!).

As we have seen in our study, the infilling of the Holy Spirit was often accompanied by speaking in tongues. If you would like to receive this gift, ask for God's Spirit to give you this prayer language. There will be time in a few minutes for us to do this. You will stay in complete control, able to start or stop when you choose. If you don't want to receive the gift of tongues nobody will force you. Then open your mouth and make sounds; continue to make sounds until the sounds become a language. This often takes some time. You'll need to practise using the gift each day. Children take a long time to learn to speak fluently, it takes a while to get fluent in your new tongue too.
7 *Believe* that you have received the gift of the Holy Spirit (Mark 11.24). (No matter what you feel.)
8 *Thank God* for his gift. 1 Thessalonians 5.18–19.
9 *Be on your guard against temptation.* When Jesus was filled with the Holy Spirit at his baptism, he was then tempted by the Devil (Luke 4.1–2). The temptation may be to doubt the whole thing and think you made it all up.

BEING FILLED WITH THE HOLY SPIRIT

20 minutes

It is now time to invite people to receive prayer for the infilling of the Holy Spirit. Here are some additional notes for mentors; depending on the circumstances, it may be helpful to invite one or two additional mentors to assist with prayer at this point. It may be most appropriate to separate into small groups so that everyone can receive personal attention from someone who has already been filled with the Spirit. If additional mentors are coming in at this point ensure that they are familiar with the steps above and are briefed in the following simple process:

1. Avoid praying with one person on your own. In particular, adult males should avoid being alone with girls in a prayer and counselling situation. Threes or fours are a good number.
2. Avoid lengthy counselling situations. The course is not designed for therapy. If issues emerge which clearly require in-depth counselling, refer to the person responsible for pastoral care in your church.
3. When somebody indicates they want prayer for the infilling of the Holy Spirit, go through the different steps on how to be filled with the Holy Spirit gently, making sure each step is understood. Check whether they would prefer to be seated, standing or kneeling. It's best to be as relaxed as you can. Do not manipulate – if they don't want to receive the gift of tongues, don't force it. Simply pray for them.
4. With their permission, lay hands on the person's shoulder or head. If it's hot and sticky, hold your hands a few centimetres away. Tell them you are going to let them pray in their own words. Pray for the Holy Spirit to fill them in your own words. If they want to speak in tongues, begin to speak quietly but audibly in tongues. Be gentle and relaxed. Stop for a few moments every now and again to encourage and reassure the person that there's nothing spooky going on. Encourage them to make sounds and to keep their mind's eye fixed on Jesus.
5. Check that he/she is praying in tongues (if desired) and let the prayer go on for a few minutes. Your group may already have experienced prayer for the filling of the Spirit, in which case you will want to adapt the ministry time, and turn it into a time of ministry for refreshing and renewing by the Spirit. Don't get too hung up teaching about speaking in tongues and don't force anyone; there is more on this subject next week.

DEBRIEF AND CONCLUSION

10 minutes

When everyone has received, invite the group to spend 5 minutes recording in their journals what has taken place in this session. If they have not finished by the end of 5 minutes, encourage them to finish off later. Conclude with a time of prayer together as is your custom, referring back to the concluding prayer time at Unit 1 if you'd like to do that prayer activity.

UNIT 4

Pneumatic drills!
(A) Gifts of tongues, interpretation and prophecy

Aims: To learn how to use the gift of tongues in personal prayer. To discover how the gift of prophecy, tongues and interpretation should be handled in gathered meetings.

PREPARATION

Invite 4 people to find Galatians 3.28, Romans 10.9, Acts 3.15, 1 Corinthians 14.2 and be ready to read these verses during the meeting.

As an experiment, invite one girl and one boy to prepare readings of some romantic love poetry, written in Portuguese, ready to read to someone of the opposite sex during the meeting. If there is likely to be any embarrassment, you could suggest that the passages are read to one of the mentors. Photocopy these passages to give to them, but ask them not to tell anyone else. The person/people leading the session may be one of the readers. (If there are Portuguese speakers in the group, you will have to make alternative arrangements.)

PASSAGE 1 (FEMALE READS TO MALE)

Beija-me com os beijos de tua boca;
porque melhor é o teu amor do que o vinho.
Suave é o aroma dos teus ungüentos,
como ungüento derramado é o teu nome;
por isso as donzelas te amam.

PASSAGE 2 (MALE READS TO FEMALE)

Se tu não o sabes, o mais formosa entre as mulheres,
sai-te pelas pisadas dos rebanhos,
e apascenta os teus cabritos junto as tendas dos pastores.
As eguas dos carros de Farao
te comparo, o querida minha.
Formosas são as tuas faces entre os teus enfeites,
o teu pescoco com os colares.

If at all possible, ensure that there is someone present who has been gifted with prophecy and interpretation before. If this is not in any of the mentors' experience, invite your minister to approach someone to help you for this gathering. It is impossible for this manual to cover every scenario that might develop; therefore it is preferable to have an experienced hand on board – not to run the meeting, but to be there in support and to help interpret what is happening should this be needed.

REVIEW

15 minutes

Review what has happened during the week; invite people to remember what happened last week and to mention anything from their Journal readings that has made an impression; conclude by asking these questions:

- Was anyone tempted to think that last week's experience was a load of rubbish?
- How have you used the gift of tongues during the week?
- Has anyone noticed themselves getting more fluent in their prayer language?
- Has anyone noticed any effects in their lives as a result of using this gift, or as a result of prayer for the infilling of the Holy Spirit?

THE GIFT OF TONGUES IN PERSONAL PRAYER

Our first aim tonight is to understand why we are given the gift of tongues and how this gift is properly used.

20 minutes

MISUNDERSTANDINGS

Remind people of the *Journey to the Eye of the Storm* idea. There have been all sorts of storms in the Church about the use of the gift of tongues. This is because of misunderstandings and bad information being passed around.

Read out the following statements and ask people to do a thumbs-up if they think they are *true*, a thumbs down if they think *false*, and thumbs sideways if they are not sure.

1 Christians who speak in tongues are more spiritual.
2 You can't be a Christian unless you speak in tongues.
3 Tongues involves a trance-like state.
4 Tongues died out after the first century along with other spiritual gifts.
5 Speaking in tongues is making mere meaningless noises.

Explain why each statement is false.

1 There is no distinction between Christians; invite someone to read Galatians 3.28.
2 A Christian is not defined by his/her gifts or attributes but by faith and witness; invite someone to read Romans 10.9.
3 Peter made it quite clear at Pentecost that the Apostles were in full control of their faculties when they were speaking in tongues; invite someone to read Acts 2.15. Paul makes it clear that, 'the spirits of the prophets are subject to the control of the prophets', 1 Corinthians 14.32.
4 Throughout the history of the Church, there have been occasions when the gift of tongues has been given. In the twentieth century this has been more common. There is no evidence from the New Testament that the spiritual gifts were only intended for the early church.
5 The opposite is the case! 'Tongues' is a language of prayer. Invite someone to read 1 Corinthians 14.2.

Why Tongues? Have 1 Corinthians 14 open throughout this section. Ensure that everyone has access to the text. Where a verse is mentioned it refers to a verse within this chapter.

The gift of tongues is a prayer language given by the Holy Spirit to help us pray (v. 14). When we pray in tongues, the Holy Spirit is praying through us; on our own, our prayers are far from perfect.

THE PERSONAL USES OF TONGUES

1 For adoration. Sometimes words can dry up and we are not sure how to tell God we love Him. After saying, 'We love you, we worship you, we adore you' a hundred times, it may all sound very much the same! Our prayer language expresses our sense of wonder, adoration, awe and love – 'mysteries with the spirit'(v. 2).

In order to get to know someone, we need to spend time with them. When we form a specially close friendship, gestures and actions can communicate as much as words. Praying in tongues is a way of spending time with God and so allowing our relationship with him to grow in depth and intimacy.

Paul also speaks of 'singing with my spirit' (v. 15). He is probably referring to singing in his prayer language as a way of expressing worship. Ask if any one has done this or heard this; have a brief discussion about the sounds people have heard and the atmosphere created by 'singing with the spirit'.

Notice that Paul does not use tongues exclusively (v. 15). He also prays with his mind. Jesus reminded us that the first great commandment is to 'Love God with all your heart, soul, strength and mind.' It would be a mistake to fail to pray in your own language even though you may have the gift of tongues.

2 For Intercession. Often we are invited to pray for someone who we may not know well. On other occasions, we are asked to pray for a situation where we are not aware of all the facts. Praying for a war zone or someone in a distant place is difficult if we don't have up-to-date information. Romans 8.26 states that we need help in our prayer lives: 'Likewise the Spirit helps us in our weakness; for we do not know how to pray as we ought, but the Spirit himself intercedes for us with sighs too deep for words.'

3 For spiritual strengthening and building up (v. 4a). When you pray in tongues you make contact with God so you are personally strengthened as a result. Often our thoughts, feelings, stresses and tensions are a barrier preventing us from coming into the presence of God. Praying in tongues may be a helpful way to begin a time of personal prayer, especially if we are stressed, tired, guilty or unhappy deep down. We will be calmed down and will probably find we have to confess sin or turn over our worries and cares to God.

THE PUBLIC USE OF TONGUES, INTERPRETATION AND PROPHECY

Now introduce the passages of romantic love poetry as follows:

20 minutes

We're going to do an experiment; two people have something important to say to two others in the group. This is not a religious statement or activity here – just an experiment for the group to observe! Please observe carefully.

Have the prepared girl read Passage 1 to one of the males in the group and the prepared boy vice versa with Passage 2. They may choose to be as romantic and inspirational as they like. A flower or a small box of chocolates would add to the flavour of the experiment.

PASSAGE 1 (FEMALE READS TO MALE)

Beija-me com os beijos de tua boca;
porque melhor é o teu amor do que o vinho.
Suave é o aroma dos teus ungüentos,
como ungüento derramado é o teu nome;
por isso as donzelas te amam.

PASSAGE 2 (MALE READS TO FEMALE)

Se tu não o sabes, o mais formosa entre as mulheres,
sai-te pelas pisadas dos rebanhos,
e apascenta os teus cabritos junto as tendas dos pastores.
As eguas dos carros de Farao
te comparo, o querida minha.
Formosas são as tuas faces entre os teus enfeites,
o teu pescoco com os colares.

Once the readings have been completed, ask the recipients of the poetry some questions.

- How did you feel when the person was reading to you?
- What do you think they were saying?
- What feelings were expressed in the poem?
- Would you like a translation of what they said?

Ask the rest of the group if anyone has any idea what was being said there. Now explain that you will read the translations.

- Passage 1 is Song of Solomon 1.2–3.
- Passage 2 is Song of Solomon 1.8–10.

Ask the group if they see the point of the experiment, which was to show the futility of people failing to communicate in a language which is not understood. The beauty and richness of the feelings were not fully understood in the experiment.

Explain: Wouldn't it be sad if lovers could not communicate to one another because of language? The message of their love would never be fully transmitted (despite what other methods they'd find to communicate their love!). God wants us to know his love in our hearts, but desires to speak to us in a language we'll understand. Where the gift of tongues is concerned, there is a difference between the private and public use of the gift of tongues. In gatherings, the gift of tongues may be used with the gift of interpretation to bring a word from God to the assembled people. The effect of this is similar to the gift of prophecy (v. 5).

Paul makes it quite clear that the gift of tongues in a Christian gathering should only be used in conjunction with an interpretation (vs 6–13 and v. 27). This is because nobody will have a clue what is being said unless there is an interpretation.

SOME GUIDELINES FOR MESSAGES OF PROPHECY OR TONGUES WITH INTERPRETATION

1. They are for strengthening, encouraging and comfort (v. 3) – that's why it's no good if people can't understand what's being said!
2. They should be in agreement with Scripture. God has revealed his will in Scripture. 'Weighing carefully what is said' (v. 29) includes holding up the prophecy in the light of Scripture as well as thinking about how the words may apply to individuals or the whole gathering.
3. There should only be two or three of each per meeting (vs 27, 29). The reason is obvious; if you're expected to weigh up what is said you'll get 'prophecy overload' if there are too many inspired words. This limit also provides some control over the Corinthian nutters who wanted to have prophecies and tongues but nothing else!
4. Only one person at a time should speak (vs 30–32).
5. Prophecy is inspired 'forthtelling' of the word of God; this may sometimes include 'foretelling'.
6. No prophecy is perfect (1 Corinthians 13.9). Especially when you're beginning to be used by God in interpretation or prophecy, you're allowed to make a mistake! Getting it wrong is part of learning.
7. 1 Corinthians 12.28 and Ephesians 4.11 indicate that some are called to be prophets. These people are likely to have frequent revelations from God (see Agabus: Acts 11.27–28 and Acts 21.10–11). Just like everyone else, these people need to be accountable to leadership in the Christian community. History is littered with the stories of prophets who went off the deep end and became arrogant because they failed to take any notice of supportive and wise leaders.
8. Prophecies may come in various forms. The Old Testament prophets sometimes spoke in visual images, stories or did a physical action to reveal what God was doing. Sometimes they spoke to individuals and sometimes to groups. A prophecy or interpretation may come as ideas, impressions, pictures, verses of Scripture, statements.

Check that everybody understands these points. Discuss any questions that are raised or fears that are lurking.

LISTENING FOR A WORD FROM GOD

30 minutes

Guide the group through these steps to listening.

- In order to begin to put into practice what has been learned, it is important for everyone to get tuned in to God. Remind everyone of the steps towards being filled with the Spirit. When Paul encouraged the Ephesians to 'Be filled with the Spirit' (Ephesians 5.18), he meant that they should go on being filled with the Spirit again and again.

Everyone should spend a few minutes quietly adoring God in their prayer language, then ensure that they are filled with the Spirit once again. (See Unit 3 for a reminder.)
- Now the group should choose to seek God and invite him to speak to them. Paul encourages the Corinthians to desire the greater or higher gifts, especially prophecy (vs 1 and 39, also 1 Corinthians 12.31). However, don't fall into the trap of seeking the gift but ignoring the giver. Jeremiah prophesied: 'Then you will call upon me and come and pray to me, and I will listen to you. You will seek me and find me when you seek me with all your heart' (Jeremiah 29.12–13).
- Invite someone to pray out loud on behalf of the whole group to ask God to speak to you all.
- Invite people now to be still and to listen; remind them of Psalm 46.10: 'Be still and know that I am God.'
- After a few minutes of quietness, encourage anyone who has a word, an idea, a verse of Scripture, a picture, an impression or a message in tongues forming in their mind to say it out loud. If someone speaks in tongues wait for the interpretation.
- After someone has spoken, look up and weigh up what has been said, while keeping a humble and prayerful attitude so as not to break the atmosphere of listening.
- Repeat the process two or three times. Don't worry if nobody says anything. Enjoy the time in the presence of God.

DEBRIEF AND CONCLUSION

15 minutes

Talk for a few minutes about what went on. Ask people to raise questions they might have and say how they felt. Then invite the group to spend 5 minutes recording in their journals what has taken place in this session. If they have not finished by the end of 5 minutes, encourage them to finish off later. You've probably done enough praying for tonight, so say a brief closing prayer of thanks for the group and end the meeting there

UNIT 5

Pneumatic drills!
(B) Gifts of healing, faith and miracles

> Aims: To role play and discuss a healing story from Acts. To apply the gift of faith by praying for healing for one another.

In this meeting the young people are going to have the chance to pray for healing for one another. You will need to look through these notes carefully and work out what is going to be the best way to encourage your group to do this. If this is all new to the young people, then they are likely to feel self-conscious and awkward, so make sure you give time to talking it through with them, and finding ways to help them through this valuable ministry.

PREPARATION

1 Get several members of the group ready to read the Scripture references that are mentioned in the Introduction.
2 Photocopy the role cards and get people from the group to play the roles of the characters in the role play on Acts 3.1–16. This does not have to be a Cecil B. deMille version of the story. It is simply to demonstrate actively what took place in the incident in such a way that group members will stay awake and take notice.
3 Have a short rehearsal before the meeting so that everyone can feel confident about what they have to do. To rehearse (you'll need about half an hour at least), read the story in Acts 3.1–16. Distribute the role cards to the people who have agreed to take part. At least two onlookers are required, but you can include more if you prefer. Photocopy the number of onlookers' role cards you require. Everyone reads their role cards to one another. Now improvise the action; here is a suggested outline of the dramatic sequence of events.

- Some onlookers carry the disabled beggar to the Beautiful Gate and leave him there for the afternoon's begging.
- The beggar begs from other onlookers who are arriving at the Temple.

- Switch to Peter and John approaching the Temple and discussing the time of prayer.
- The beggar asks Peter and John for money.
- Peter and John stop and look at the beggar.
- Peter speaks to the beggar.
- Peter stretches out his hand to lift the beggar.
- The beggar stands and feels the strength come into his feet and ankles.
- The beggar begins to walk then starts to leap around shouting thanks and praise.
- Onlookers see and hear the beggar jumping around.
- They are stunned and check with one another whether they are seeing things.
- Totally amazed, they run over to Peter, John and the beggar to ask how it all happened.
- Peter quietens them and tells them the words of verses 12–16.

Practise the action a few times through until everyone is sure of what to do. Peter may read the speech in verses 12–16, but he must read it clearly so everyone can hear. Some humour may be valid but should not be an end in itself; avoid turning the whole thing into a joke!

If there is absolutely no possibility of a rehearsal before the meeting, choose the 3 people who are most likely to be good at improvising and get one of the mentors to do a brief 15-minute rehearsal with them at the start of the meeting, during the Review time. In this case you may have to help them considerably when it comes to the question and answer time.

4 Photocopy the questions and have them available to distribute to group members before the role play.

5 Discuss responses to the questions with the role players. The clues to all the answers are in the role cards and in the text Acts 3.1–16. John and Peter may like to refer to some of Jesus' healings in the Gospels. In addition, check out Luke 10.9; Mark 16.18; Acts 1.8; John 14.12–14.

Role cards

Role cards for the characters of the beggar, Peter, John and onlookers follow on pages 33 and 34.

THE BEGGAR

You have been disabled since birth, unable to walk so unable to work. You have developed a career as a beggar and you regularly go to the Beautiful Gate at the Temple to ask the passers-by for a handout. You have some good friends who carry you there every day at three in the afternoon just as people are going in for their afternoon time of prayer. You ask Peter and John for money and they respond by looking straight at you. Then Peter tells you to stand up and walk and reaches out to lift you up by the right hand. For the first time, your feet and ankles can bear your weight, so you begin to walk; then you jump up and down with delight, yelling out praise and thanks to God while holding on to Peter and John.

PETER

You are walking to the Temple with John, your young colleague. As you go through the Beautiful Gate, a beggar asks you for money. You don't have any just now, but you stop and look at the beggar and you tell him to look at you. The memories of how Jesus used to heal the sick flood into your mind, as do his promises that you would do what Jesus used to do and his command that you and your colleagues should heal the sick. You are filled with faith because you have seen the risen Jesus and you know that the same Spirit who raised him from the dead is alive in you. Then you address the beggar: 'Silver and gold I do not have, but what I have I give you. In the name of Jesus Christ of Nazareth, walk.' You reach your hand out and lift the beggar up to his feet. And he walks! Just like you told him to! When the people come running over in amazement to see the disabled man, you have to give an explanation. Your explanation is Acts 3.12–16.

JOHN

You are with Peter going up to the Temple in the afternoon for prayer. As you are passing the Beautiful Gate you are stopped by a beggar on the street who asks you for money. You find yourself looking straight at the beggar, just like Peter. As Peter addresses the beggar, you find yourself agreeing with every word he says; as you remember how Jesus used to heal the sick and how he promised and commanded that you should do the same, you believe without any doubt that the risen Jesus whom you have seen has come to you in his Spirit and that he is going to do the same through you and Peter as he always used to. When Peter speaks in Jesus' name it is as though Jesus himself really is there, so you don't doubt that the man is going to be healed. You stay with Peter and the healed beggar, amazed and thankful that Jesus is still alive, through you and the other disciples. You're happy for Peter to do all the talking, but you keep praying and praising quietly throughout the whole episode remembering that Jesus told you, '...anyone who has faith in me will do what I have been doing'.

ONLOOKERS

It's prayer time in the Temple. You make your way through the usual assortment of people to get to pray. It's your habit. The disabled man at the Beautiful Gate is there as he has been for years, asking for a handout. Just as you're getting ready for the time of prayer, you hear a commotion in the Temple courts. Someone is shouting at the top of his voice praising and thanking God. Most unusual for anyone to get so excited! You look over to see what's going on and recognize the disabled beggar jumping up and down with delight. You're amazed! He's healed! You run over to the beggar and ask all sorts of questions to find out whether you're seeing things. Has he been a fraud all along? Perhaps he has a twin brother? How come he's on his feet? Did he just get a nugget of gold or a kilo of silver? Why is he so boisterous? Then you see he's holding on to a big fisherman-type and his young colleague so you ask them for an explanation. You listen to the answer with amazement.

Questions

TO PETER
Why did you choose to heal the beggar instead of walking past as you must have done many times before? Why did you speak to the beggar in the name of Jesus Christ of Nazareth?

TO THE BEGGAR
How long had you been disabled? What do you think happened to you that you were able to walk? Why did you go around leaping and praising God?

TO JOHN
What were you thinking when Peter began to speak to the beggar? Why did you and Peter have faith to believe that the beggar could be healed?

TO THE ONLOOKERS
What did you think when you saw and heard the disabled beggar shouting and jumping around? How can you be sure that the healing is genuine and not a fraud? Is this going to affect the way you think of Jesus Christ? Was Peter's explanation of the healing convincing? What did he say that particularly stuck in your mind?

REVIEW

15 minutes

- Review what people remembered from last week.
- Ask what people have read during the week from their journals and whether anyone has something to share.
- Remind the group of the *Journey to the Eye of the Storm* idea.

INTRODUCTION

5 minutes

Introduce the theme of this Unit: gifts of faith, healing and miracles. Paul lists these three gifts together, with FAITH as the common feature to gifts of healing and miracles. He is speaking from the experience of years of being used by God to perform miracles and healing. Later he was to remind the Corinthians of this: read 2 Corinthians 12.12.

By FAITH, he has in mind something different from the act of faith that someone makes to become a Christian: read Romans 10.9. The gift of faith is given for a specific situation, where human efforts are insufficient. We'll focus particularly on the gift of healing in this unit and the relationship of faith and healing gifts. The word for 'miracles' is the same as that which describes the miracles of Jesus; it may refer to nature miracles and exorcisms.

The Letter of James describes 'the prayer of faith' as being the key to healing in the local church situation: read James 5.13–15.

While anybody can pray for healing, some are particularly gifted. Just like tennis! Anyone can hit a ball over the net, but professional tennis players are specially talented. Equally, like tennis, the gift needs to be developed. No tennis player can win a Grand Slam event without training, practice and usually plenty of losses on the way. Similarly, those who are gifted as healers usually take time to develop and grow in understanding, application of their faith and their ability to tackle the more serious illnesses.

We will look at one healing incident in the New Testament, then some principles from the Bible we can put into practice in growing the faith that is required to exercise gifts of healing. In all this, we need to remember one vital factor; God wants a relationship with us. God is not like the cosmic bell-boy who comes running at our bidding when we press the right bell. We cannot see healing simply as a mechanical process. More than anything, God invites us into the intimate friendship of Father, Son and Spirit; in that intimacy and love is the power to heal.

The key to the gifts of healing, faith and miracles is your relationship with God. Seek the Giver primarily, not the gifts.

THE ROLE PLAY ON ACTS 3.1–16

25 minutes

Tell the group that this is an enactment of a biblical story and the aim is to discover what the story can teach us about the gift of healing. Explain that there are a number of questions to be asked of the characters in the role play and invite group members to look at the photocopied questions. Encourage everyone to think of further questions to ask during the presentation.

Encourage the group to pay attention to the role play and to encourage the participants by keeping still and not interrupting the presentation. Suggest that appropriate laughter and applause at the end are allowable.

Present the role play. After this, the questions may now be asked. Ask each one in turn of the character concerned. The role players should stay out in the front remaining in role as the characters they have been playing.

When each of the prepared questions has been asked and responses have been given, invite the group members to ask any further questions of the characters. The mentors may assist in the responses at this point if necessary.

CHOOSING A HEALING PROJECT

40 minutes

We have been looking at the story of how Peter and John first chose a healing project. In their direct confrontation with illness, they exercised the gift of faith and the healing of the disabled beggar followed immediately. In one sense, you might think that Peter and John had some advantages over us. After all, they'd seen Jesus heal; they'd listened to him command and promise that they should do the same; they saw him crucified and then recognized him in his risen body; what's more, they were there at Pentecost when the building shook, the wind of the Spirit blew, the fire of God's Presence fell and they were gifted with tongues. After all that, they certainly would have had huge reason for faith enough to get someone healed. It is interesting that this healing created a storm for Peter and John; they were thrown into jail! (Acts 4.3)

On the other hand, we have some distinct advantages too. Remember what Jesus said to Thomas after the resurrection? Thomas didn't believe Jesus was risen until he saw him personally. Then Jesus told him, 'Because you have seen me, you have believed; blessed are those who have not seen and yet have believed.'

The other good news is that we don't have to be spiritual giants with enormous faith; Jesus preferred people who were honest about their faith. A concerned father came to Jesus requesting healing for his son. 'Everything is possible for him who believes,' Jesus told the father. 'I do believe; help me overcome my unbelief!' was the father's immediate reply. Jesus healed the son (Mark 9.23-24). When the apostles said to Jesus, 'Increase our faith!', Jesus replied, 'If you have faith as small as a mustard seed you can say to this mulberry tree, "Be uprooted and planted in the sea," and it will obey you' (Luke 17.5-6).

Our faith will only grow as we exercise it. We are going to choose a healing prayer project relevant to the faith we have. If it's less than a whole mustard seed's worth, let's choose a small project to begin with.

Jesus has the power to heal. When he announced the Kingdom of God, he showed that this Kingdom was to bring us wholeness and peace by healing those who were sick, giving joy to those who were miserable and making friends with the unloved. Jesus unleashed waves of God's healing compassion. Now he has ascended into Heaven, he has unleashed his healing compassion in the Church. The power to heal is available; God's Spirit has been given for his people to connect with God's compassionate flow of healing and so bring his healing to the world.

What must we do? To turn on a radio programme, we have to plug into the power source, switch on the power and tune in to the wavelength. It's the same with the power to heal.

Go through this process of preparing for and doing the Prayer of Faith. Then, when everyone is clear on how to do it, do it! It should take about 10 minutes to go through the 3 stages, leaving you 30 minutes for exercising prayers of faith.

STAGE 1: GETTING ON THE WAVELENGTH
Follow the same pattern as in Units 3 and 4, remembering that Paul encouraged us to 'Be filled with the Spirit and go on being filled with the Spirit.'

STAGE 2: ASKING FOR GOD'S POWER
Ask God to put his healing energy into you. It's a quite logical request, for Jesus commanded and promised his disciples that they should heal. Say a prayer such as, 'God, please increase in us your life-giving power to heal; come to us now to heal, Holy Spirit.' Now wait for a while expectantly and let God breathe his power and life on you.

STAGE 3: RECEIVING GOD'S POWER
Believe that the power is coming into you and accept it by faith. After all, you tune into your favourite radio station because you believe that someone is transmitting on that wavelength. If there are no blockages, God is transmitting his healing energy, because Jesus said he would;

say 'Thank you' in faith. 'Thank you that your life and healing energy is coming into us now increasing life in our spirits, minds and bodies. Keep coming, Holy Spirit.'

CHOOSE

Now's the time to be specific – time to make a choice about praying for physical healing. The group should choose to pray for someone who is not completely well. At any time, people are on medication for small illnesses – coughs, colds, flu, viruses; some may be suffering from headaches, stomach aches, strained or twisted ligaments or other injuries. It is better to start on something small that may well get better anyway, but which could do with some prayer to speed up the healing. As you get more confident in the prayer of faith, you can take on bigger projects. Invite anyone to request prayer for themselves or someone they know who is not well.

When someone in the group requests prayer (for themselves or someone else), then you can focus on that person by laying on hands. Two or three people may lay hands gently on the shoulders and head; others stay close by with hands stretched out touching those who are praying. As you are connected to the power and compassion of God, so his healing energy will flow through your hands into the body of the person for whom you pray.

SEE

First of all, as you pray, picture the person totally healthy. This gets our spiritual creativity going. Let the mind dwell on this picture of total well-being; it may be helpful to speak in tongues quietly as you create this healthy mental picture. Imagine the light and life of God flowing into the area of the body which is unhealthy and glowing in and around it.

SPEAK

Next it is necessary to speak out loud the prayer of faith and assert the word of power, 'In the name of Jesus Christ, let this be so.' The act of speaking in faith is a creative act of power. God spoke and said, 'Let there be light!' And it was so. The centurion whose servant was sick knew the creative, healing power of the word of Jesus: 'Speak the word only and my servant shall be healed' (Luke 7.7). Whenever Jesus healed, he spoke the word that brought into being a living, healing energy flowing from his body into that of the sick person and restoring them to health.

Having exercised faith by speaking the creative word of healing in the name of Jesus, stay there with hands laid on for a while and let the healing life soak into the person. Keep the creative mental picture of health going and keep praying gently in tongues. Just as the healing power is flowing mysteriously through your hands, so the same life-giving energy is sent through your tongue, even though you may not understand the words.

When you have finished, you may have time to pray for someone else. Alternatively, if there are several more requiring healing prayer, you may need to form two or three smaller groups. This whole section should not take up more than 30 minutes, for healing prayer is exhausting and hard work.

DEBRIEF AND CONCLUSION

15 minutes

Talk for a few minutes about what went on. Ask people to raise questions they might have and say how they felt. Then invite the group to spend 5 minutes recording in their journals what has taken place in this session. If they have not finished by the end of 5 minutes, encourage them to finish off later. You've probably done enough praying for tonight, so say a brief closing prayer of thanks for the group and end the meeting there.

UNIT 6 Pneumatic Drills! (C) Gifts of Knowledge, Wisdom, and Discernment

Aims: To discover what Paul means when he refers to these three gifts. To practise seeking God and listening to God.

PREPARATION

5 minutes

Ensure that there are enough Bibles for everyone to have one. Three groups will be created. These will need photocopies of the relevant group instruction sheet. They will also need pens and paper. Mentors should workshop the exercises with the 3 small group facilitators beforehand.

If at all possible, ensure that there is someone present who has been gifted with words of knowledge before. If this is not in any of the mentors' experience, invite your minister to approach someone to help you for this gathering. It is impossible for this manual to cover every scenario that might develop; therefore it is preferable to have an experienced hand on board – not to run the meeting, but to be there in support and to help interpret what is happening should this be needed.

REVIEW

10 minutes

- Review what people remembered from last week.
- Ask what people have read during the week from their journals and whether anyone has something to share.
- Remind the group of the *Journey to the Eye of the Storm* idea.

INTRODUCTION

5 minutes

Knowledge, wisdom and discernment are three ideas that belong very much together. Being wise and discerning, with the resources of great knowledge acquired through years of experience, is something few of us can boast of! However, Paul states in 1 Corinthians 12 that the Holy

40

Spirit graces individuals in the Body of Christ with words of wisdom and knowledge as well as the ability to discern the spiritual source of behaviour and actions.

So what's the difference between these three gifts? Rather than give definitions, we'll have a look at different stories in the New Testament that show these gifts in operation. Then we can see the purpose and function of each; this will give us some understanding about how the Holy Spirit may choose to operate in giving wisdom, knowledge and discernment.

However, let's be clear that all the gifts of the Spirit are gifts! Remember from Unit 3 that Paul encourages the Corinthians to desire the greater or higher gifts, especially prophecy (vs 1 and 39, also 1 Corinthians 12.31). However, don't fall into the trap of seeking the gift but ignoring the giver. Nowhere does the Bible say, 'If you shall seek the gifts you shall find them!' Rather, the Bible keeps encouraging us to seek the Giver.

Jesus said: 'Seek first the Kingdom of God and his righteousness and all these things shall be added...' (Matthew 6. 33). (Reminder from Unit 4:) Jeremiah prophesied: 'Then you will call upon me and come and pray to me, and I will listen to you. You will seek me and find me when you seek me with all your heart' (Jeremiah 29.12–13).

Jesus is the source of wisdom, knowledge and discernment. Jesus has become for us the Wisdom of God (1 Corinthians 1.30). Over 700 years before the birth of Christ, Isaiah prophesied of Jesus:

> The Spirit of the Lord will rest on him –
> the Spirit of wisdom and understanding,
> the Spirit of counsel and of power,
> the Spirit of knowledge and of the fear of the Lord –
> and he will delight in the fear of the Lord. (Isaiah 11.2–3)

Jesus invites us into the same relationship with the Father that he knew. 'If anyone loves me, he will obey my teaching. My Father will love him, and we will come to him and make our home with him' (John 14.23). To discover how the three gifts operate, we will create three groups – Wisdom, Knowledge, Discernment – and invite each one of them to tell the stories they will research and comment on the gifts mentioned. There will be some background information and a series of questions to guide your comments. The groups will do the following research:
1 Find the Bible passage concerned. Invite someone to pray that this activity will enrich your relationship with Jesus.
2 Read the passage together. It will be really helpful to 'jam' it as you did in Unit 2. This will help you to hear the story in a fresh way.
3 Appoint one or two spokespersons who will record the answers to the questions raised and inform the other groups of your discoveries.

4 When the groups come together, the spokeperson(s) will tell the story you have read and explain how it is an example of the gift in question.

SMALL GROUP WORKSHOPS

WISDOM GROUP INSTRUCTION SHEET
Luke 19.47—20.8. (See also Acts 6.8–15 and 1 Kings 3.16–28).

30 minutes

1 Find the Bible passage concerned. Invite someone to pray that this activity will enrich your relationship with Jesus.
2 Read the passage together. It will be really helpful to 'jam' it as you did in Unit 2. This will help you to hear the story in a fresh way. Don't forget the 3 stages of the process. Read around the group a verse at a time; read around the group giving the text away; read around the group taking the text from the previous person. Then you are ready for full jamming. (Check Unit 2, if you need a full description of the process.)
3 Appoint one or two spokespersons who will record the answers to the questions raised and inform the other groups of your discoveries.
4 When the groups come together, the spokeperson(s) will tell the story you have read and explain how it is an example of the gift in question.

Background information
- John the Baptist had earlier been beheaded, much to the satisfaction of the chief priests and teachers of the law.
- John had been very popular, so the people were hugely disappointed when he was executed. They believed he was a prophet.
- The teachers of the law and chief priests wanted to trap Jesus so that they could arrest him.
- When asked trick questions, Jesus frequently raised an alternative question to get through to people's hearts. In this case, the 'Word of Wisdom' was Jesus' question in verse 4. This 'Word of Wisdom' contained sharp wit.

Questions
1 Why could the religious leaders not answer the question Jesus asked? (See vs 5–6.)
2 How do you think the religious leaders felt when Jesus outwitted them? (Vs 26 shows the result of a similar attempt to trap Jesus.)
3 Do you think they learned anything? (See vs 19, 20.)
4 What was the source of Jesus' sharp wisdom and wit?
(See John 3.34–35.)

Now read Acts 6.8–15. (No need to jam it; get one person to read it to the rest of you.) Note verse 10. This is a fulfilment of Jesus' promise to the disciples in Matthew 10.17–20, 'When they arrest you, do not worry about what to say or how to say it. At that time you will be given what to say, for it will not be you speaking, but the Spirit of your Father speaking through you.' Following this, Stephen stood up to defend himself. While his wisdom and strength were outstanding, his message was unpopular; he was stoned to death.

SOME CONCLUSIONS

These two instances are examples of Words of Wisdom. Particularly when we do not have huge natural resources of wisdom to deal with difficult questions and opposition, there is a promise from Jesus that the Holy Spirit will give us the right words to say. The key is to stay close to the Father; if our relationship with God is broken, we cannot hear his words.

In the Old Testament, Solomon had a Word of Wisdom when confronted by two mothers each claiming to be parent of one baby! See 1 Kings 3.16–28 for clarification.

About Wisdom in the Bible:
- Wisdom is creative. The Word, through whom all things were made (John 1.1–3), is often associated with Wisdom.
- The Wisdom of God is based on the Cross of Christ. It looks weak and foolish, but is effective in restoring people to friendship with God (1 Corinthians 1.20–25).
- The Word of Wisdom has great power, as shown by the examples given. The religious authorities had their motives exposed by Jesus and therefore had the chance to repent; likewise, the enemies of Stephen. Solomon's word of wisdom was effective in bringing a fair result to the women's dispute.

Warning

The promise of Jesus to give words of wisdom is no excuse to avoid the hard work of 'wising up', by studying the Scriptures and thinking through difficult questions about your faith. The Word of Wisdom is also the ability to apply what we know to a particular situation or issue. The Holy Spirit may remind us of what we have already learned or understood to enable us to respond to somebody's question or problem.

KNOWLEDGE GROUP INSTRUCTION SHEET
Acts 10.9–23
1 Find the Bible passage concerned. Invite someone to pray that this activity will enrich your relationship with Jesus.

2 Read the passage together. It will be really helpful to 'jam' it as you did in Unit 2. This will help you to hear the story in a fresh way. Don't forget the 3 stages of the process. Read around the group a verse at a time; read around the group giving the text away; read around the group taking the text from the previous person. Then you are ready for full jamming. (Check Unit 2, if you need a full description of the process.)
3 Appoint one or two spokespersons who will record the answers to the questions raised and inform the other groups of your discoveries.
4 When the groups come together, the spokeperson(s) will tell the story you have read and explain how it is an example of the gift in question.

BACKGROUND INFORMATION
- The earliest Jewish Christians thought that people had to become Jews before they could become Christians. It was a big surprise that God should speak to Cornelius, a Roman.
- When Peter went up to the roof he'd have been hungry and resting under a canopy to shelter from the sun. The vision God gave to Peter stemmed from his immediate surroundings (the roof-top) and experience (he was hungry).
- In Peter's vision there was a mixture of clean and unclean animals. Orthodox Jews were forbidden to eat certain meats, so this mixture of animals would have disgusted Peter.
- Peter received two types of revelation: (a) the vision and (b) the voice (vs 19–20).
- Peter had a clear understanding that he had to change his mind about the differences between Jews and Gentiles. (See v. 28.)

Questions
1 What was Peter doing to prepare himself to be open to hear God? (See v. 9.)
2 Did Peter immediately understand the vision? (See v. 17.)
3 How did Peter respond to the Spirit's prompting? (See v. 21.)
4 How did Peter treat the people who had arrived at Simon's house? (See v. 23.)

SOME CONCLUSIONS
Words of knowledge may come in different ways; Peter received both a vision and some clear, unmistakeable words of instruction. Visions (e.g. Ezekiel ch. 37), dreams (e.g. Joseph – Genesis 37), pictures (e.g. Peter in this passage), instructions (e.g. Peter in this passage), parables (e.g. Nathan the prophet – 2 Samuel 12), an audible voice (1 Samuel 3), a physical action (Agabus in Acts 21.10–11) are among the various

ways God chose to give revelation in the Bible.

The way words of knowledge are received is likely to be in keeping with the individual's personality and experience. Peter was challenged by this vision to change his views about the Gentiles because of the various animals in the vision. This was appropriate for him because he was a Jew.

Words of knowledge require Wisdom to understand what to do with them. Peter's understanding of what God had revealed to him came later after he had met with Cornelius' messengers.

Paul wrote, 'Knowledge puffs up, love builds up.' Watch your pride! Joseph was unwise to tell his dream to his brothers; his pride brought him trouble! Remember 1 Corinthians 13, the Love chapter.

DISCERNMENT GROUP INSTRUCTION SHEET
Acts 16.16–24. (Also Mark 2.1–12.)

1 Find the Bible passage concerned. Invite someone to pray that this activity will enrich your relationship with Jesus.
2 Read the passage together. It will be really helpful to 'jam' it as you did in Unit 2. This will help you to hear the story in a fresh way. Don't forget the 3 stages of the process. Read around the group a verse at a time; read around the group giving the text away; read around the group taking the text from the previous person. Then you are ready for full jamming. (Check Unit 2, if you need a full description of the process.)
3 Appoint one or two spokespersons who will record the answers to the questions raised and inform the other groups of your discoveries.
4 When the groups come together, the spokeperson(s) will tell the story you have read and explain how it is an example of the gift in question.

Background information
- Paul and Silas were in Philippi where they had begun to tell people about Jesus.
- The slave girl had no freedom; she was owned both by slave-masters and the spirit of 'divination'.
- Paul was troubled (v. 17). This was the gift of discernment operating in him. You might have thought that what the slave girl was saying was to Paul's advantage. However, Paul discerned that the source of the girl's shouting was a spirit within her.
- Discernment enables a decision to be made about the source of someone's behaviour. There are three alternative sources:
  a) The Spirit of God;
  b) A person's own thoughts, ideas and will;
  c) The Devil.

Questions
1 Once Paul had discerned the spirit in the girl, how did he respond? (V. 18.)
2 What was the result of Paul's response? (V. 18.)
3 If you knew that you would be arrested, beaten and jailed for doing what Paul did, would you have done it? Why or why not?
4 Who won in the struggle between Good and Evil in Philippi? (Read vs 25–34.)

Now read Mark 2.1–12 (no need to jam it; get one person to read it to the rest of you). Note v. 8. In his spirit, Jesus discerned what they were thinking. Perhaps their faces or body language showed some disapproval of what Jesus had said; however, there is more than common sense or guesswork in what Jesus knew in his spirit.

SOME CONCLUSIONS
- The gift of discernment is given by the Spirit but this does not deny the need for reason and common sense.
- Some Christians go over the top and start finding demons behind every coffee cup. This is to be avoided, because it diverts our attention onto the Devil. Jesus rose from the dead to demonstrate that he has won victory over the Devil. The focus of our attention needs to be on Jesus. He will grant the gift of discernment freely when and as necessary.
- If you are in Christ, the Devil is under your feet because God has placed all things under Christ's feet (Ephesians 1.22). Therefore, remain in Christ.
- The most common discernment required is to check whether an idea, word or revelation is from God or not. Sometimes it might simply be the bright idea of the person speaking! Always check whether the content of the message is in accordance with God's revealed will in the Bible.

TAKE A BREAK

5 minutes

Allow people a 5-minute break because they've been concentrating hard in small groups. Everyone should get up and walk around or stretch, to be ready to listen carefully to one another during the presentations.

PRESENTATIONS

15 minutes

Each group will have 5 minutes to tell the story they have researched and give a brief explanation of the gift in question.

LISTENING FOR A WORD FROM GOD

25 minutes

Guide the group through these steps to listening:
- In order to begin to put into practice what has been learned, it is important for everyone to get tuned in to God. Remind everyone of the steps towards being filled with the Spirit. When Paul encouraged the Ephesians to 'Be filled with the Spirit' (Ephesians 5.18), he meant that they should go on being filled with the Spirit again and again.
- Everyone should spend a few minutes quietly adoring God (suggest they use their prayer language quietly if they have received tongues) then ensure that they are filled with the Spirit once again. (See Unit 3 for a reminder.)
- Now the group should choose to seek God and invite him to speak to them.
- Invite someone to pray out loud on behalf of the whole group to ask God to speak to you all.
- Invite people now to be still and to listen; remind them of Psalm 46.10: 'Be still and know that I am God.'
- After a few minutes of quietness, encourage anyone who has a word, an idea, a verse of Scripture, a picture, an impression or a message in tongues forming in their mind to say it out loud. If someone speaks in tongues wait for the interpretation.
- After someone has spoken, look up. Weigh up what has been said, while keeping a humble and prayerful attitude so as not to break the atmosphere of listening.
- Repeat the process two or three times. Don't worry if nobody says anything. Enjoy the time in the presence of God.

DEBRIEF AND CONCLUSION

10 minutes

Talk for a few minutes about what went on. Ask people to raise questions they might have and say how they felt. Then invite the group to spend 5 minutes recording in their journals what has taken place in this session. If they have not finished by the end of 5 minutes, encourage them to finish off later. You've probably done enough praying for tonight, so say a brief closing prayer of thanks for the group and end the meeting there.

Warning! Young people are often more open to hearing the voice of God than adults who have been conditioned in the Christian Church not to expect God to speak to them! Therefore, it is right to foster the environment in which young people may listen. However, it is also worthwhile to be wise and discerning!

There are real dangers possible when so-called words of revelation deal with directions about young people's parents, career or potential partners. Mentors should be particularly aware of this and use their own judgement and common sense if these issues arise.

Beware of the ego trip! Some may well receive a genuine word of revelation but later begin to think that they know everything! Encourage humility and assure everyone that no special degree of holiness is bestowed on those who are given gifts. 1 Peter 5.5–6 is a good reference point and reminder.

Note on Units 7–10: The weekend

A detailed timetable of a whole weekend of structured activity is not presented here. The 4 units of study are described in detail, but these should take place in the context of a relaxing, fun time. The following times are recommended for the units:

Unit 7: .... 60 minutes on Friday evening
Unit 8: .... 100 minutes on Saturday morning
Unit 9: .... 60 minutes on Saturday evening
Unit 10: .... 60 minutes on Sunday morning

Units 7 and 8 run into each other, so if things are not finished by the end of Friday night, don't worry. After both Units 9 and 10, time should be allowed for worship and prayer ministry.

UNIT 7

The Tertius Diaries

Aim: To prepare, enact and debrief a simulation based on Paul's first letter to the Corinthians.

The church in Corinth was in a bit of a mess. That's why Paul needed to write letters to the Corinthians, to get them to sort out their confusion and return to order. Every community goes through chaos and has to deal with differences among its members. That's part of becoming a genuine community. In the first letter to the Corinthians there are some helpful guidelines for all churches, particularly to enable communities to use the spiritual gifts in a constructive way.

Units 7 and 8 are designed to help people work through the problems faced by the Corinthian Christians. Many of their mistakes have been repeated down the ages, and many are still being repeated today. The exercise is designed not only to underline the correct use of spiritual gifts but also to help people understand the processes and feelings involved when a church drifts into chaos. It's a fairly sure bet that all the young people involved in *Journey to the Eye of the Storm* will one day face issues of conflict in the church.

During the exercise, the mentors will need to guide the process gently but firmly. Detailed knowledge of 1 Corinthians 12 and 14 is essential to this part of the journey. Participants should already have been placed in 4 separate groups by the mentor. Ensure that everyone has at least one good friend in each group, but also ensure that you don't reinforce the development of exclusive cliques. Have the butcher's paper and markers ready for the groups to take.

INTRODUCTION

5 minutes

Tonight and tomorrow morning we will be doing a biblical simulation. This is where we all put ourselves into the shoes of some of the people described in the Bible and try to understand more of what the Bible teaches as a result. Tonight and first thing tomorrow is the preparation stage; then we move into the simulation itself; then we have a Debrief time to work out what we have learned.

This simulation is entitled *Chaos in Corinth*. Our aim is to learn the principles taught in 1 Corinthians of dealing with disorder among Christian people and to be involved in the experience of sorting out disorder.

For the simulation we will divide into 4 groups. These are:
1 The Tertius Group
2 The Chloe Group
3 The Erastus Group
4 The Paul Group

Each group has two background sources:
1 Source A The Tertius Diaries have been leaked to the press. Tertius gives a frank account of what's going on in the Corinthian church.
2 Source B Group role description. This describes the points of view of your particular group.

The Paul Group also has a third source. This is Paul's first letter to the Corinthians, which we imagine has not as yet been written, but represents the thinking that Paul has done in response to the issues raised in the Tertius Diaries.

GROUP TIME ON THE TERTIUS DIARIES

20 minutes

Your task is to gather together in 4 separate groups and read the Tertius Diaries out loud. As you are reading, make a list of each problem that you hear which Tertius identifies. When you have agreed on the list of problems, note which of these problems are also happening today in the life of the Christian Church, as far as you are aware. Give examples where you can without getting personal or turning the exercise into gossip. Be prepared to come back after 20 minutes and appoint a spokesperson to explain your lists which will be posted up for everyone to see.

When the groups have formed, let them go into their own space, but warn them 5 minutes before time is up.

FEEDBACK TIME

Each group displays its lists and a spokesperson explains them.

10 minutes

GROUP TIME ON ROLE DESCRIPTION SYMBOL DESIGN

15 minutes

Now give the further instructions.

In the next group sessions you will be given the second source – your group's role description. Read through the role description and check that everyone understands it. Your task then is to agree on a symbol which represents the group role and points of view described. Using the markers and butcher's paper, draw this symbol and appoint someone to explain why this symbol has been chosen. This is so that each group's identity and viewpoint will be recognized by the others when it comes to the discussion time.

FEEDBACK TIME

10 minutes

Each group explains its symbol. The mentor then explains that tomorrow's session will feature a council meeting between representatives of the various groups to discuss the question, 'Should we ban the use of spiritual gifts for a while in order to restore order to the church in Corinth?'

The Tertius Diaries

A storm has been brewing among the Christians in Corinth! It is about time that things got sorted out and we began to live at peace with one another again. I am hoping that Chloe and Erastus will agree to visit Paul with me so that he can help us get it right. We were always told that Christians were meant to get along with one another, but in Corinth we spend the time upsetting each other! It's all gone sour!

Let me explain. I am Tertius. I work as a secretary-slave in the city of Corinth. I have been educated by my slave-master so I know how to think; I can read and write. It isn't easy being owned by somebody else, but I'm fortunate to be well treated, unlike some of my friends.

Corinth is full of cheats, philosophers and abusers. In commerce, there is plenty of ripping-off; in public debate there are loads of stuck-up big mouths; in relationships, slave-masters are frequently unkind and women are often treated badly. Many people here live in fear, trapped by systems that make their lives miserable.

That's why Paul's teaching about Jesus was so attractive to us. We used to dream of a world where men and women were to be treated equally and where slaves could be respected the same as slave-masters. Slaves used to dream of being able to teach their wisdom and insights to others in words that ordinary people could understand. Paul came along speaking about this kind of world in language that made sense; he said Jesus had lived and died and risen to destroy the old world and start a new one.

Some of us were convinced when we saw healings happen among us. When disease was driven from people's bodies, Paul told us that this was a sign of God's rule. We couldn't argue with that; we thought it was better to be ruled by this sort of God that by the rip-off merchants, liars and abusers of Corinth; many of us joined the Christians.

But people don't change altogether overnight! For 18 months Paul had held meetings in the house of Titius Justus, next door to the Jewish synagogue. Crispus the synagogue leader joined us and Erastus the city treasurer became part of our group too. Many of my friends couldn't believe that I was associating with those high-class people in my leisure hours; they came to have a look and have become Christians. So we have all sorts among us – well-educated important folk; middle-class people; uneducated workers, rich and poor, men and women, slaves and free people.

When Paul left, an Egyptian guy called Apollos took over leadership for a while. He was different from Paul; very eloquent and quite long-winded. Some Christians joined us from other places; they claimed to have known Peter – The Rock – who was a close assistant and friend of Jesus himself. Now we have people with one-eyed loyalties to these various different leaders. Do you see the problems? Some people claim they belong to Apollos, some to Peter, some to Paul, some to Christ! They don't want to be a community at all. Just a bunch of separate small groups.

Since everyone can receive the spiritual gifts (even the uneducated!), everyone wants to do their own thing. Nobody listens any more. We have people speaking in tongues all the time; several people prophesying all at once; people claiming to have words of revelation; people wanting to be heard and recognized for how specially gifted they are. Some people like to have the spiritual gifts happening all the time; others prefer some reasoned teaching. Those who've been educated like to listen. Those who don't write and have never had any education prefer to get their knowledge straight from God, so they like prophecies and tongues and spiritual experiences all the time.

I've brought my friends to the meetings and some of them think we're mad. Last month there was chaos. Some of the women were prophesying all evening and refusing to listen. I couldn't understand what they were saying. Some were speaking in tongues and my friends were laughing because nothing made sense. We couldn't even hear Apollos speak and Gaius, who owns the house where we meet, was getting most upset.

My friends recognized some Christian colleagues who'd been visiting prostitutes the week before. 'I thought you said these people were different,' they taunted. Worse still, they recognized people who were suing one another in the public courts. 'This lot are the same as everyone else; fighting with one another; out for themselves alone; I don't know why you bother,' commented my friends.

The greatest embarrassment was over the food. I'd told them that we had a shared meal, when we all remembered Christ and everyone took bread and wine together to show we were united. When we arrived, the food was all gone and some of my fellow-believers were staggering around drunk. 'If we'd wanted to picnic and booze, we could have gone out on the town,' my friends told me.

The next time they came, there was food enough – but it was meat that had been sacrificed to the goddess Isis. You could buy this meat cheaply in the market. Some of the Christian slaves had learnt that Isis and the other gods were not real, so they felt it was okay to buy the sacrificed meat. My friends just joked that they were Isis-worshippers; they couldn't understand how we claimed to worship Jesus Christ but seemed to allow Isis-worship as well.

Needless to say, my friends don't intend coming back! I really don't blame them. We've been very inconsistent. Our actions have not matched our claims that Jesus has brought in a new kind of world. We quarrel and fight in public and in private; we have people who are grossly immoral; we separate into different groups; there's chaos when we meet together; we have problems of leadership; some of the women remain uptight; the poor slaves who get heard nowhere else can't keep quiet and go over the top.

Despite all this, we are glad to be numbered as Christians. We have known the presence, peace and power of God's Spirit among us. We've seen people healed; we've seen people grow in confidence; people who were called useless by society have been recognized as valuable; people who have done all kinds of wrong have been touched by God's Spirit; they have known they've been forgiven so have made friends with their enemies; Gaius, Crispus and Erastus have become my friends even though they are from a different class of people; the slaves among us know they are as gifted as anyone.

Most of all, we each know that God has made us his adopted children. We have each known the Spirit of God within us making us want to shout out, 'Dad! Father!' We know for sure that Jesus has risen from the dead because we're not afraid of death any more. Each of us has received personal evidence from God's Spirit that the story about Jesus is true.

We're in the midst of a storm just now. We hope we will be able to settle our differences, but we need some advice and courageous leadership to sort things out. Maybe then even our storm will be a help to churches in the future when the people argue and fight with one another. Our hope is that if we tell Paul the plain facts, he'll be able to respond with clear and practical guidelines so that all of us will behave properly and be at peace with one another again.

A MEMBER OF CHLOE'S GROUP (SEE 1 CORINTHIANS 1.11)

You are rejoicing in your new-found freedom. All your life you have been bossed around. Now you are realizing your self-worth; you are one in Christ with all the rich and influential people of the church in Corinth. That means you are a somebody! Not a nobody!

Hands have been laid on you and you have received the gift of the Holy Spirit; you're sure of that. You and your friends have been struck by your new status. Even you can receive inspiration from the Spirit of God.

Gifts of tongues, prophecies, interpretations, visions, understandings; even though you've had no education, you and your friends are not short on divine manifestations. You can't read and you don't always understand the teachers in your church, but you can bypass all of that by getting ideas, visions, words straight from God's Spirit. You've heard somewhere that God's Spirit must not be quenched, so you want more and more of the specially inspired prophecies, interpretations, visions, words especially from those in your close circle of friends.

You are, however, very concerned about the divisions that exist in the church. The personality cult of following a particular teacher is too much and you think that ill-feeling will continue. Nevertheless, you are fed up with people who are greedy and irresponsible. You work hard all day, but when you go out to be with your fellow Christians you find that they don't care enough to leave you any food! This frequently makes you angry.

You believe that:

1 The greedy people should be severely ticked off.
2 Women should be free to dress as they like and speak as they like in church meetings since there is no distinction between the status of men and women in the Christian Church.
3 Spiritual gifts should be encouraged more than dry teaching.
4 Free expression should be given to emotion in worship.
5 The past personal history of individuals should not be held against them; tolerance should be shown to those whose lives are not yet perfect.
6 Everybody should have the opportunity to speak in the church meetings.

ERASTUS

You have worked hard all your life and have arrived at a position of power and prestige in the city administration of Corinth. However, the arrival of Paul in Corinth some time ago changed your life completely. Your friend Titius Justus invited you to his house to hear what Paul had to say and you found this preacher so convincing that you became a Christian.

For over a year you learned as much as you could. You took to the road for a while to accompany Paul in his work. You travelled with Paul's sidekick Timothy to establish the Christian church in Macedonia. (See Acts 19.22 and 2 Timothy 4.20.)

You have carefully learned a body of teaching from Paul. You and Tertius, a secretary, have discussed this teaching in great detail and it is part of your life. You consider that it is your responsibility to pass on this teaching about the work of Christ to others in Corinth. However, they don't always want to hear. They are more concerned to gabble away in tongues, sing loudly and enthusiastically and get carried away with the excitement and emotion of the worship. You are not always impressed with the group of slaves who generally refuse to listen to you. The problem is, if you say anything too strict they misinterpret you; they think you are using your social standing to boss them about.

Another problem in the church is with sexual immorality. Frankly, you think that some of the Corinthians should be put out of the church for their sexual misconduct. You think that Paul will agree with you on this.

And the women are so talkative! Some even refuse to wear headgear on the pretext that 'the men don't and we're all one in Christ.' Such behaviour is quite shameful in your view; but again, you are likely to be misinterpreted if you are too firm in stating your opinions.

You believe:
1 Order must be restored in church meetings.
2 Emphasis must be given to proper teaching about the faith.
3 Spiritual gifts should be discouraged in order to quieten some potential troublemakers who may wrongly bring false teaching.
4 Sexual deviants should be driven out of the church.
5 The law should be used to drive unwanted people away. Sue them!
6 Women should sit at the back quietly out of the way.
7 Those who don't make it to the shared meals on time shouldn't complain if the food is gone.

TERTIUS

You were Paul's personal secretary-scribe when he was in Corinth. You helped him prepare a long and profound letter to the Christians in Rome (Romans 16.22). You are one of those people who gets to know everyone and everything that's going on. You make it your business to find out what is happening to everybody else. You work for Erastus in the city administration and you know Paul's mind and character pretty well.

Chloe is a good friend, but you get upset by some of her associates. They are uncouth and uneducated and you hope that they will learn to better themselves. You and Chloe are also concerned by the way people gather around particular personalities. There is constant bickering between the Paul-ites, the Peter-ites, the Apollos-ites and those who claim, somewhat proudly, to be followers of Christ alone.

You have some good friends whom you would like to introduce to Christianity. But what will they see if they come along to the church in Corinth? You are worried that they'll see and hear some very strange things – much speaking in tongues, perhaps some disorderly behaviour, maybe some drunkenness. They may meet people with dubious reputations. If only you could hide that man who is living with his stepmother! What an embarrassment if he should be there! After all, you've been trying to tell your colleagues why the Christians show restraint in matters of sexual relationships.

However, it's good that you'll be able to introduce your friends personally to such influential people as Erastus, Gaius and Crispus. In fact, that's a big bargaining chip for you. Your colleagues eye you with some suspicion when you mention names like this; but it does provoke interest!

You believe:

1 The church must be more concerned with its mission to the city of Corinth than with its petty divisions.
2 Embarrassment will be the result if things carry on as they are; outsiders will be put off; they'll just think Christians are mad.
3 People need to be brought together to agree with one another.
4 Christianity must appeal to people's minds as well as bring about changes in people's lives.
5 The uneducated people should be included and tolerated but not allowed to run the whole meeting.

PAUL

Erastus, Tertius and a member of Chloe's group have decided to sort out some of the differences in the Corinthian church by setting up a meeting with you. They have come to you for advice about how to restore order and harmony in the church. They are hoping that your advice will be clear, concise and acceptable to all the different groups within the church. Although they are each concerned about the divisions within the church, each of them has different views. Each wants to bring these views to you who will listen to their stories.

Many people in Corinth have questioned whether you really are an Apostle; some remember that, as Saul, you used to throw Christians into jail and have them beaten. Hence, you are sometimes on the defensive with these people. Frankly, these Corinthians are often a headache to you and you need to be quite firm with them.

Your task is to listen to all the difficulties of the church in Corinth and to give the people sound, reasonable and godly advice. You remember that in Jerusalem you once spoke with James, the leader of the church there, who told you that God's wisdom is first of all pure, then peaceful, gentle and easy to please, always ready to help those who are troubled and to do good for others. It is always fair and honest. This is how you will aim to behave.

To understand the issues that Paul has to deal with read through 1 Corinthians 14. (With regard to verses 34–36, see the section at the beginning of the mentor's notes. Also look up Acts 18.1–11 which relates what happened when Paul first went to Corinth. Paul was the one who brought Christ there in the first place.) Note carefully the following principles from the chapter which need to be communicated in the meeting:

1 Love is the key objective.
2 Spiritual gifts are to be desired, especially prophecy.
3 There is a difference between tongues and prophecy.
4 Spiritual gifts are for strengthening the church.
5 Everyone may make a contribution when meeting together, but in an orderly way.
6 No more than two (or at the most three) messages in tongues.
7 Ensure that tongues are interpreted.
8 If no interpreter is present, tongues-speakers should pray quietly.
9 Prophets may speak one after the other – again no more than two or three.
10 Don't ban speaking in tongues, but keep things in order.

UNIT 8
Chaos in Corinth

> Aim: To prepare, enact and debrief a simulation based on Paul's first letter to the Corinthians.

INTRODUCTION

5 minutes

A reminder about the background to the simulation. A meeting has been called by three different groups within the church at Corinth. Paul has been invited to attend to bring his wisdom and insights even though he is not universally accepted in the church.

There are three phases in the simulation process:

1 Preparation: 25 minutes to choose 3 people from the group to represent your perspective.
2 Simulation: The meeting to discuss the question: 'Should we ban the use of spiritual gifts for a while in order to restore order to the church in Corinth?' The meeting may go on for up to 40 minutes.
3 Debrief: After a break, there will be a further 30 minutes to debrief, identify what has been learned and record findings in the journals.

PREPARATION

25 minutes

The mentor checks out the role of Stephanas. (See 1 Corinthians 1.16; 1 Corinthians 16.15–16.) Instruct each group as follows:

Your task is to prepare your ideas for the meeting that will shortly take place. Appoint someone to lead the group during the preparation. Re-read your role description and note carefully your group's views in relation to
1 The spiritual gifts issue
2 Other problems that have been identified in the Tertius Diaries.

Three of you should be chosen to sit in on the meeting. Of the remainder, one should be appointed a chronicler; that is, someone who will take notes on the discussion, watching carefully how people seem to feel, what they are saying and how the group seems to become more or less healthy in the process. Another should take the role of 'Time Out' Caller. If you feel the members of your group need some reminders about the views they should represent you may call 'Time Out' once during the meeting. You then have up to 3 minutes to discuss things in your group.

Rules of the simulation:
1 Chair: Stephanas will chair the meeting. He will introduce himself at the beginning of the meeting.
2 Seating: groups will be seated in a semicircle. Members of each group will sit together. Additional group members will sit behind the semicircle.
3 Time Out may be called once by each group for up to 3 minutes.
4 If there is no agreement on the main issue, a vote may be called by the Chair.
5 The Chair will decide who speaks. No speaker should go on too long, or the Chair may courteously conclude the speaker's time.
6 The Chair will end the meeting after the appropriate length of time.

THE SIMULATION

40 minutes

The mentor introduces Stephanas and proceeds to the chair in that role. Care is taken to encourage as many as possible to participate. Leading questions may be asked of particular participants to get the discussion going. The simulation is introduced as follows:

We have gathered today to discuss the question, 'Should we ban the use of spiritual gifts for a while in order to restore order to the church in Corinth?' We welcome everybody and invite you to introduce yourselves and bring your opinions about this matter.

At the end of the simulation, thank everybody for their participation and close the meeting. A break should be taken and the chairs rearranged for the debrief so that everybody is in a circle.

DEBRIEF

20–25 minutes

The mentor guides the discussion, once again ensuring that as many voices are heard as possible, one voice at a time. Here are some suggested discussion starters and questions.

- Invite the chroniclers to say what they observed during the discussion.
- Invite participants to say how they felt during the meeting.

- Who called 'Time Out' and why?
- Ask members of the different groups if they were satisfied that their views were heard.
- What was the decision of the meeting?
- What is the likely outcome to be for the church in Corinth?
- Was the decision in accordance with biblical principles as described in 1 Corinthians? In what way? Check that everybody hears what these principles are.
- What was learnt about the way to deal with conflict?
- What did anyone else learn from doing the simulation?
- How do people feel about this as a way of applying what the Bible says?

JOURNAL TIME

5–10 minutes

Invite everyone to have a few minutes on their own recording what has taken place and praying on their own for wisdom to put into practice the biblical principles for behaviour that have been discovered.

UNIT 9 Crazy mirrors or God's mirror? The Holy Spirit and self-image

Aim: to recognize where we get our self-image from and exchange our own distorted views with our Creator's view.

PREPARATION

Invite people to look up the Bible references that are mentioned in the course of this talk. Then write up the questions for discussion during the Discussion time. Have them ready to be uncovered at that time.

INTRODUCTION

5 minutes

The connection between the rest of the course and this session is the theme of *giftedness*. Getting a right self-image will enable us to become the people God created us to be, freely exercising and developing our giftings.

Ask if anyone has been into a 'crazy mirror' hall where all the mirrors distort the images. Ask what the images looked like and what the experience of seeing crazy views of yourself was like. Life is a bit like a Hall of Crazy Mirrors. How do I look at myself? Where do I get my self-image from? Is my view of myself true, or is it distorted, like in one of those crazy mirrors? Do I agree that, since God knows and sees everything, his view of me is likely to be more true than my own view of myself? Which is more healthy to have – my own view or God's view of me?

Tonight, our aim is to recognize where we get our self-image from and exchange our own distorted views with our Creator's view. Not only is each person gifted with natural talent, personality and skill, each person *is* a gift, designed and given by God to the world.

The world is full of Crazy Mirrors which surround us every day. There is another mirror we can look into – the Bible, which says how God sees us. Jesus' second great commandment is 'Love your neighbour as yourself.' Yet how can I love my neighbour if I don't love myself? Self-love is not like Narcissus! He was the guy who thought he was so beautiful, he spent the whole time looking at himself in the reflection of a lake – until he fell in the lake, couldn't swim and drowned!

DISTORTED IMAGES OF OURSELVES

10 minutes

Some of the Crazy Mirrors which reflect back to us what we feel we are like make impressions on us which affect the way we behave. Here are some examples:

A 3-year-old boy moved overseas to live. Because of jet-lag he kept waking up in the middle of the night wanting to play. While his mum slept, his uncle awoke, smacked him, told him he was a naughty boy and sent him back to bed. Over the next few days, the little boy became unhappy, and started to behave in a very anti-social way. He wanted attention and did all he could to get it. When his cousin built a sandcastle he jumped all over it, destroying all his cousin's work; at the table he threw the sugar across the room. Eventually he was asked, 'Why are you doing these things?' by his mother. 'Because I'm a naughty boy,' was the reply. He had believed the reflection his uncle gave him of what he was like and behaved accordingly.

At school, Bill was always told he was useless at academic work. His teacher convinced him that he had no future in staying on at school. He left school as soon as possible and took up an apprenticeship on the railways as a painter. When he was called into full-time Christian ministry later on, he had to study for academic qualifications. He was motivated to succeed and worked hard. After 7 years of part-time study, he was awarded a university degree – some 25 years after he had left school believing he would never succeed academically. He had believed the reflection of himself given by a discouraging teacher and followed a career path accordingly, until his own view of himself was changed by God's call on his life.

Shelley was shy and introverted at high school and not very attractive in either looks or personality. She fell ill and was away from school for a few days. While she was away, a teacher arranged for a social experiment. The other students were encouraged to treat Shelley as though she was one of the most attractive people in the class, both for her appearance and character. Everyone agreed. In a few weeks, Shelley had become far more confident and began to take a lot of care in how she looked. Before long, she had become popular and good-looking; it wasn't hard for the rest of the class to continue to be friendly and warm towards her. Her view of herself had been changed by the way she was treated.

When Christopher Columbus wanted to sail west to find the new world, he had the greatest difficulty in raising finance and a crew for the voyage. The reason for this was that both financiers and sailors believed that the earth was flat! They thought that when Columbus reached the edge of the world he and his boat would fall off, losing lives and financial investments. The whole world was in a 'cultural trance' which affected how everybody believed and behaved. Today newspapers, TV, magazines and movies impart a view of what a real Man or a real Woman should be like. This holds us in a cultural trance.

He is a big success in business with recognition, respect, a big home, gold credit cards, hot cars, exotic holidays and unending talent. He's a great athlete, strong and handsome, but sensitive and caring too. His rippling muscles, winning ways and huge heart have made him a lover to be coveted, a guy who's been chased by the girls since primary school.

She is equally talented and successful with an executive career and immaculate clothes. She's top of the list for society parties, she's beautiful, modern, liberated, in control and oozes sex appeal. Independent, intelligent and chic, she drives a flashy sports cabriolet and is constantly dining with the stars in the most expensive restaurants.

Male or female, the media condition us to strive for this ideal. When I don't measure up to the image the world has of what I ought to be like, I feel I'm somehow not good enough; I'm no longer free to be the person God created me to be. I need to break out of the cultural trance.

A golfer was always terrified of the eighth hole, especially the lake beside the fairway. The ball would always end up at the bottom of the lake although his mind was saying, 'Watch out for the lake, watch out for the lake!' Actually, the golfer's subconscious was so directed onto the lake, that the swing of the club automatically sent the ball into it! Deep down, the golfer believed that he wasn't talented enough to avoid the lake, so his behaviour acted in accordance with his level of self-belief.

GOD'S MIRROR

10 minutes

The big question is, 'How do I trade in my self-image and get a new one?' 'Therefore, if anyone is in Christ he is a new creation; the old has gone, the new has come!' (2 Corinthians 5.17). It is the birthright of everyone who is a Christian to get a new self-image. A choice has to be made to believe God's mirror – the Bible – rather than the distorting mirrors of the world. God's mirror reflects to me three things to believe about myself:

1 CREATED!

I am made in God's image. Read Genesis 1.26, 27 and 31. God does not make garbage! God likes what he has made. He delights in what he has created. I am the pinnacle of God's creation.

God has very carefully designed me: 'See, I have engraved you on the palm of my hands...' (Isaiah 49.16). God knows everything about me:

> O Lord, you have searched me and you know me.
> You know when I sit and when I rise;
> you perceive my thoughts from afar.
> You discern my going out and my lying down;
> you are familiar with all my ways. (Psalm 139.1–3)

Certainly, our sin has spoiled the image of God in us. The hurt done to us by other people may also scar and stain us. We need forgiveness and freedom from trying to be what other people think we ought to be.

Imagine a sculptor who works to create a beautiful sculpture. She is invited to place the sculpture in a public park where people can appreciate and admire it at their leisure. As time goes by, the sculpture is damaged. People ride by on motorbikes, splashing up mud and dirt. Pigeons fly overhead – you know what they do – splat! Vandals come by and hack into the sculpture with knives.

A year later the sculptor comes to look at her sculpture once again. She sees her creation spoiled by mud, bird droppings and vandalism. What does she do? Destroy the sculpture? Of course not! She spent years on this work of art; she knows and loves her creation! She gets out oil and a rag and cleans the sculpture; she gets out a knife and carves it carefully again where it was damaged. In the end, her creation is just as beautiful as it was before. She has re-created it.

2 RESCUED!

If I were the only person in the world who had turned their back on God, Jesus would still have to rescue me from the clutches of sin. I have been rescued from the penalty of sin: 'For the wages of sin is death, but the gift of God is eternal life in Christ Jesus our Lord' (Romans 6.23). I am being rescued from the power of sin: 'For we know that our old self was crucified with him...so that we should no longer be slaves to sin' (Romans 6.6). I will be rescued from the presence of sin: 'But now that you have been set free from sin and have become slaves to God, the benefit you reap leads to holiness, and the result is eternal life' (Romans 6.22).

Imagine you are a life-saver at the beach. It is a windy, rainy day and the waves are choppy. Suddenly you spy something bobbing up and down 30 metres out to sea. It is a child in great difficulty. What do you do? You swim out to sea and rescue the child. You're a hero! The photographers from the local paper all come down to take your picture!

Next day you're down at the beach again. The wind is howling even more, the waves are higher, the rain is pouring down. You spy something 40 metres from the shore. It's plastic, it's brown, it's a garbage bag bobbing up and down. What do you do? You stay on the beach of course! You don't risk your life to rescue garbage.

If God had thought I was garbage, Jesus Christ would not have bothered to die for me. Because God places uncountable value on everyone, Jesus has bothered to rescue each one of us – even me. I have a choice – I can struggle against my rescuer if I wish and reject the offer of a free rescue.

3 FILLED TO OVERFLOWING!

'"If anyone is thirsty, let him come to me and drink. Whoever believes in me, as the Scripture has said, streams of living water will flow from within him." By this he meant the Spirit, whom those who believed in him were later to receive' (John 7.37–38). This is the promise of Jesus. His Spirit will overflow out of anyone who puts their trust in him.

Very often our self-image expresses itself as fear; I am afraid of what I appear to be. However, the infilling of the Holy Spirit changes that: 'For you did not receive a spirit that makes you a slave again to fear, but you received the Spirit of sonship. And by him we cry, "Abba, Father". The Spirit himself testifies with our spirit that we are God's children' (Romans 8.15–16).

The truth is that, so long as we remain in Christ and are being filled with his Spirit, we 'are being transformed into his likeness with ever-increasing glory, which comes from the Lord, who is the Spirit' (2 Corinthians 3.18).

Created, rescued and filled to overflowing! If I believe that, my self-image will change and I will be free to be the person God made me.

JON'S STORY

5 minutes

Jon is 20 and comes from Kirkby in Ashfield. His story is an example of how a new self-image may emerge in the person who gives himself to Christ. Here Jon reflects on how, during 1995, the Holy Spirit changed him from being shy, introverted and withdrawn to a person so filled with confidence and poise that he's able to play front man in youth club events which regularly draw 250-300 young people.

'The Holy Spirit and me. When did it all begin? How did it all begin? I can't really remember; all I can say is how much of a difference it has made in my life. I am now doing things I never imagined doing and in fact things I never really wanted to do.

I started university last year and I really hated it. I had a lot of trouble making friends because I was so shy. This was made worse when my girlfriend dumped me and I felt very alone. I had nothing in life to aim for and I felt lonely and unwanted. I felt really sorry for myself for many weeks until I decided that I wanted someone to pray for me.

What a change! It wasn't instant, but after getting prayed for quite a lot of things began to change. As people prayed for me my body began to do things it had not done before. I would fall over, bounce up and down in a pogo-like manner, shake for long periods of time. It didn't just end there though, my confidence grew and I began to come out of myself.

As I look back I can see how much of a difference God has made in my life. It hasn't always been easy and I still get times when I feel down, but I have far more good times than bad. God has turned what looked like the worst year of my life into probably the best.'

DISCUSSION

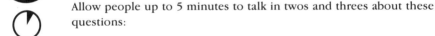

Allow people up to 5 minutes to talk in twos and threes about these questions:

5 minutes

1 What struck you most about the talk?
2 What did you learn about yourself from the talk?
3 What did you learn about what God does?

JOURNAL TIME

5 minutes

When the discussions have finished or when 5 minutes are up, invite everyone to record their main impressions of the talk in their journals. Suggest that they might like to record how they intend to respond to God as a result of hearing the talk. If they finish before the others, invite them to respect everyone else's journal time and pray quietly.

PRAYER MINISTRY

20–30 minutes

When 5 minutes are up, it's time to pray. Lead this time with the mentor's assistance. The mentor will take over at any time if you're not sure what to do.

If you sing together, have some worship at this point to draw you into God's presence. Then invite the Holy Spirit to come to do his transforming work among you. You may find it helpful to repeat the process of being filled with the Spirit as in Unit 3. Wait in God's presence, then pray for one another, expecting the Holy Spirit's power to be released among you. Be free to exercise any of the gifts of the Spirit as they are inspired. Encourage people to request prayer from others. If they simply wish to receive more of the Spirit of God to change them more into his likeness, invite people to raise their hands so that two or three others can pray for them.

UNIT 10

'You are gifted!' Identifying, owning and developing natural and spiritual gifts

> Aim: To begin planning a public event to share with others what has gone on during *Journey to the Eye of the Storm*. In the process, to identify, develop and affirm the giftedness of the people in the group.

A mentor will lead this session in conjunction with a group member to get the ball rolling efficiently and thoroughly, especially when it comes to making decisions about the presentation.

INTRODUCTION

10 minutes

Christian disciples are not made simply to receive good gifts but to be:

1 Witnesses

Jesus promised the disciples, 'But you will receive power when the Holy Spirit comes on you; and you will be my witnesses in Jerusalem, and in all Judea and Samaria, and to the ends of the earth' (Acts 1.8).

2 Servants

As a senior disciple, Peter advised others, 'Each one should use whatever gift he has to serve others, faithfully administering God's grace in its various forms. If anyone speaks, he should do it as one speaking the very words of God. If anyone serves, he should do it with the strength God provides, so that in all things God may be praised through Jesus Christ' (1 Peter 4.10–11).

God's purpose in gifting us is to release us into a life of witness and service. He has given us the power to do this, so we need to co-operate with him by becoming co-creators and co-workers with him.

It is right for us to plan together to tell people what has happened to us over the past few weeks. We will each be doing this among our own friends, but there is a special strength when we combine our gifts and prayer for united witness and service. We need to work out what to do, when and how to do it and who we'd like to invite.

Unless the group chooses to do something totally different, it is recommended that you put on an Eye of the Storm Banquet to which you will invite guests, give them a brilliant meal, entertain them and inform them of what you have done and learned. This will be an act of service, in that you will be showing hospitality to your guests, and of witness, in that you will be telling them what Christ has been doing among you. However, don't make life too hard for yourselves. If the banquet is too difficult to co-ordinate, work out an achievable alternative during your brainstorm.

This is not intended to be an in-house event for the church alone. Rather, it is hoped that friends, relatives and colleagues will be invited to hear something of what God is doing today. It is therefore important in your preparations to ensure that testimonies, stories, songs etc. are not written in overly religious language which cannot be understood by outsiders.

In order to prepare, the group will have to identify the interests, gifts, talents and potential guests. The activity itself will encourage the recognition and development of individual giftings and the overall confidence of the group. If you need to use people outside the group who have specific talents, that is fine. You will need to identify someone with the gift of persuasion to convince them to take part!

GIFTS AND MINISTRIES BRAINSTORM

In groups of 4 make a list of each person's particular interests, talents and ministry motivations. Write the list on butcher's paper. Take 5 minutes per person.

20 minutes

1 Ask each person what they are interested in, what they like doing and what they believe they are good at.
2 The other people in the group then add other qualities and talents which they have observed in that person.
3 Read together Romans 12.3–7. From the list of giftings in verses 6 and 7 choose one which most excites you.

GIFTS AND MINISTRIES RECOGNITION

Come together and put up the lists of gifts and talents and ministry motivations that have been identified. Everyone goes round looking at the lists for about 10 minutes. Encourage people to be positive about one another – no put-downs allowed.

10 minutes

ALLOCATING TASKS TO BE DONE TO MAKE THE BANQUET HAPPEN

20 minutes
(then take a break and come back to it later)

Check the lists you have been looking at and, as far as possible, match up the gifts and motivations with the responsibilities to be taken on.

RESPONSIBILITIES

Guest list to be put together: Everyone has to be in this to decide who you'd like to invite. Don't forget the people who have been praying for you for the last few weeks – they'll want to hear what's been happening. Think of the people you would like to tell about Jesus – family, neighbours, friends from school or sports clubs, people you work with. Everybody should come up with a list of 3 people each.

Invitations to be designed, prepared and distributed: artistic people will be needed here together with a creative and sharp thinker to get the wording right. Honesty is essential to explain what will happen at the banquet. And who has access to a good computer with good graphic software?

Additional ways to be found to persuade people to come: are there some key peer group leaders who should be recruited to help in some way so that others will definitely come? These people don't have to be Christians – just people who are natural leaders; get them on side so that others will follow; give them a useful role to play.

Menu to be prepared: who has skills in this area?

Shopping to be done: ensure that a shopping list is brought together from all 'task' areas.

Food and drink to be prepared: who has skills in this area?

Venue to be prepared and decorated: who is good at interior design?

Waiters and waitresses to be briefed: someone will need to take responsibility to ensure they are immaculately dressed and know exactly what to do!

Programme to be organized: your aim is to tell the story of what's happened during the journey. You can tell it with music, art, drama. If you've been singing together and have musical talents, present some of the songs you've done or get someone to write a new song for the occasion. Artists could do some paintings which depict what has gone on visually. An art exhibition would be very interesting. You might like to present one of the role plays you've been doing as a dramatic feature. At least one or two should tell their stories straightforwardly of how they have become Christians and what impact the journey has made on them.

Prayer to be a major feature in preparation. Gather in twos or threes at least once a week to pray particularly for the 3 priority guests you've invited – that they will come and become Christians as a result.

Plans to be made to help nurture those who become Christians or who show interest. It will be important for you to enable people to respond to what is presented. A response card to be filled in on the night will be helpful. Plan to run a group or a weekend for those who show interest in the Christian faith.

Funds to be raised. You could write to local businesses, to the church council, to request assistance. Or plan a fund-raising event to cover the costs. Someone who is good at budgeting needs to help here. How much could people in the group contribute? You may need to ask people to consider that question prayerfully and get back to you confidentially.

Clean up to be planned – everyone can be involved in this!

Additional assistance to be recruited – check what skills you don't have covered and list possible helpers you could ask.

Conclude the session with everyone clear about what they have to do so far and agree to come back to the preparation tasks at a later stage. Commit all your preparations to God and pray for your act of witness and service together.

UNIT 11
'Tell the story!': (A) Preparation for the group's presentation

UNIT 12
'Tell the story!': (B) The presentation